Kingdom Systems Training

Wise Master Builders Mastery Course

Rodney D. Veney

Understanding Kingdom Models and how to Develop Kingdom Systems in order to build successfully in the Kingdom of God

Copyright © 2012 Author Name

All rights reserved.

ISBN:1724512080
ISBN-13:9781724512086

DEDICATION

The Wise Master Builders Mastery Course is dedicated first to my dad, Walter W. Veney, who demonstrated a level of service I never fully understood until I discovered the Kingdom of God. I honor my dad with this first publication for his endurance, a mantle which has been passed on to me. My dad's life of service continues to be a source of motivation and inspiration today and I often find myself being led to share from his life whenever I am teaching others about endurance. Dad's body of work on earth was a visual illustration of Hebrews 10:36. "For you have need of endurance, so that after you have done the will of God, you may receive the promise." When the book was about to close on dad's earthly life, I firmly believe that the only regrets he had was that he would not able to see and be part of a story that he began to write. A story that would be fulfilled through his seed in the earth. I will always remember those last visits with my dad before he transitioned as I sat there in a hospital room and watched a man who was at peace with himself and the life he had lived. My dad not only passed on to me a mantle of endurance but he also gave me a model to follow. His model has taught me how to get the job done in spite of any level of opposition or adversity and to be at peace with myself in the end.

Not much is said concerning the price children pay when the father decides to pursue destiny. Ecclesiastes 5:3 declares that a dream comes through much activity. Much of the activity required to pursue destiny can take away from time spent with children and grandchildren. Especially during the seasons of searching or when we are not quite clear on what we have been sent to do. I therefore also dedicate this publication to my daughters, Shanel and Charis. Shanel my first-born, represents strength and is a strong but quiet leader destined to lead the coming generations into a dimension of kingdom living. Charis, my youngest, represents grace and is also destined to emerge as a strong kingdom leader. Both of you, in some way, endured my years of searching and seeking for the intent of God. I honor both of you for your contribution to my ability to impact and influence the lives of many as the hard lessons I've learned in fathering each of you became the revelation used to impact and influence many of those I've mentored and coached through the course of several years of teaching and training. The kingdom of God attributes the fruit of those transformed lives to each of you. The honor bestowed here today is but the beginning of seasons of life wherein you will reap the benefits of your sacrifice. Each of you will be rewarded for your contribution and sacrifice towards the fruit of kingdom transformation in the earth. For every life that is transformed and aligned with the intent of God through reading and applying the principles taught in this book, kingdom rewards are commanded upon your lives as well as the lives of your children. The blessing of the Lord is to the 3rd and 4th generation. If the consequences of sin can be passed on to our children, so can the consequences of obedience. Shanel and Charis, receive your honor today!

CONTENTS

	Acknowledgments	i
	Introduction	3
Lesson 1	Kingdom Models	8
Lesson 2	Kingdom Systems	12
Lesson 3	Legal Requirements	19
Lesson 4	Dreamers and Visionaries	24
Lesson 5	Emerging Kingdom Leaders	29
Lesson 6	Small Vision – Small Provision	38
Lesson 7	Mantles and Motives	44
Lesson 8	Kingdom Rewards	50
Lesson 9	Giving and Receiving	55
Lesson 10	Sent Dimension	61
Lesson 11	Apostolic Order	65
Lesson 12	Multi-Dimensional Grace	73
	Conclusion	80

ACKNOWLEDGMENTS

First and foremost I want to acknowledge the phenomenal divine leadership of Holy Spirit. I acknowledge Him as the CEO of all the affairs of the Kingdom of God in the earth realm. I could not have made it this far without His divine leadership in my life. Thank you for revealing Yourself to me, guiding and directing me into greater dimensions of kingdom truth. Thank you for revealing a clear purpose and enabling me to see into the intent of the Father's heart.

Next, I would like to acknowledge my incredible family including my amazing wife Lisa, whose unwavering support enables me to remain focused and committed to the intent of God. You are one of the kindest persons on earth and your ministry of kindness passes knowledge and continues to impact and influence many beyond your ability to comprehend. You love the unlovable and show mercy to the unmerciful and your ministry is truly a labor of love. The words from Ephesians 3:19 define your service to the population at large. "To know the love of Christ which passes knowledge." I am honored to have you as my wife and partner in life.

My mother Ann, for modeling and demonstrating faith in God through the course of the years of my life. So many you did not give birth to, now call you mother or momma. Each time someone outside of our biological family refers to you as such you are being honored. Your ministry of love has crossed generational, ethnic, and religious boundaries. You are an inspiration in every sense of the word and I honor you for your contribution to my journey in life.

To my sisters, Gerald, Janet and Deborah, you'll have been such an awesome support team and each of you continues to walk with me on this journey today. I would be remiss without also mentioning the intercessory prayer team who has provided prayer support throughout the years of this journey. Rena Anderson, Hope Greene and Sandra (Gerald) Sorrell, you've all made an invaluable contribution to the success of my journey and I honor each of you for all you've done. Bertha Jackson, a longtime friend who committed her time, energy and focus to edit this course. I thank God for your literary grace. You are a true friend indeed.

Finally, I want to acknowledge all of the incredible leaders who have mentored, taught, trained and equipped me throughout the course of my journey as well as every person I've ever mentored, coached, taught, trained or equipped. I thank each of you for serving me and or giving me the opportunity to serve you. You've been instrumental in me being able to discover my gifts and grace as well as develop my craft in order to become the kingdom leader I am today.

INTRODUCTION

THE PLACE WHERE KINGS LIVE

Imagine you are boarding a plane traveling to a country you've never visited before. You know very little about this countries culture, government, laws or way of life. The plane takes off and after a lengthy flight you arrive and exit the plane. You don't know how to navigate this country. You are totally unfamiliar with this countries way of life so the first person you meet is the Royal Governor whose name is Holy Spirit. Accepting Jesus as Lord and giving Him the opportunity to Lord over your life has created the opportunity to live in this country. But now you must accept and comply with the office, function, role and assignment of the Royal Governor. Jesus told you Holy Spirit would meet you and help you navigate this country before you took flight. You must learn to totally depend on the leadership of the Royal Governor in order to navigate this country known as the Kingdom of God. No, you are not dead and this is not the heaven you were taught about in your Sunday School classes. This countries way of life creates a heaven here on earth. The Royal Governor knows everything there is to know about this country. He also knows everything there is to know about the Father's plan for your life in this country. The Royal Governor declares to you that this is the place where only kings live.

The Royal Governor begins to explain and make clear that in order to live in and enjoy the benefits of this country, you will have to learn the culture, the laws and the language of this country. This means your philosophies, belief system, value system and paradigm will all have to shift and change in order to align with the mind and intent of the Father. Your level of thinking does not work here in this country. Your thoughts and your language have been influenced by a different system. Your thoughts therefore are limited and your language is not in tune with the sound of the kingdom of God. You will have to be trained to see what the Father sees in order to honor all creation. Additionally, in order to participate in the kingdom communications system, a high level communications system that releases the sound of the will of God, you will have to redefine what you consider prayer. As the Royal Governor continues to introduce you to the kingdom of God, He explains that you have not yet truly entered the kingdom of God because you do not live here yet. In order to live here you must endure a separate process that focuses on the alignment of every area of your life with the intent of God. This alignment requires a serious commitment to a kingdom process that applies consistent pressure to each subdomain of your life. The Royal Governor goes on to explain that in order to successfully complete this process you must focus only on kingdom truth.

The Royal Governor continues to explain that it is hard for those who have established lives to enter the kingdom of God. This is not a lateral move but a start over proposition and this process of alignment will actually reconstruct entire areas of your life. In spite of the challenges that lie ahead you are excited about the journey and ready to begin. You've never seen anything like this country and you are persuaded beyond any shadow of doubt that this is where you want to live. So, you make a commitment to be taught, trained and equipped to fulfill your destiny here in this country. The Royal Governor will now lead the way into a dimension of kingdom truth that leads to a dimension of kingdom living unparalleled by any other dimension of life that could ever possibly exist. This is truly the place where only kings live.

The Kingdom of God is all about learning and in order to live in and enjoy the benefits of the kingdom of God and the life God intended for us, we have to be committed to learning and growing in the knowledge of kingdom grace. Truth is dimensional and the highest level or dimension of truth is kingdom truth. Kingdom truth brings us into a wholeness dimension where there is nothing broken, nothing missing and nothing lacking. From a dimension of kingdom truth we operate with the mindset that nothing is broken, lacking or missing in or from our lives. The only issue is misalignment with the intent of God. Every problem stems from some level of misalignment which puts us at rivalry with God. Problems and challenges in life are misdiagnosed in the absence of kingdom truth. A misdiagnosis is simply the receipt of low level truth which is categorized as bad information in the kingdom of God. We cannot successfully execute the will of God with bad information.

There are many misconceptions, wrong concepts and erroneous ideas people have concerning the Kingdom of God that must be eradicated by means of relevant kingdom teaching that challenges foundational beliefs. Many leaders who have only been introduced to the kingdom of God try to put their own spin on the kingdom of God and the kingdom of heaven suffers violence. We cannot legally force our way into the kingdom of God. In the absence of an authentic kingdom transformation process that shifts and aligns our thinking, our thoughts, our perspectives and outlook on life with the intent and will of God, we will try to make the kingdom come into agreement and alignment with our own thoughts, mind, will and intent. Talking about, teaching or preaching about the kingdom of God under these circumstances is an attempt to illegally access the kingdom of God. This is what is meant by "the kingdom of heaven suffers violence." On the other hand, you must be violent to possess the kingdom. This speaks to the tenacity that is required in order to possess the kingdom. The kingdom of God is not possessed by the casual believer or the faint in heart. The kingdom of God requires courage, tenacity, endurance, consistency, and steadfastness.

Seeking the Kingdom also requires that we take a systematic approach to learning, discovering and applying the principles of the Kingdom of God in our lives. There should be a major shift from one generation to the next that ushers in another dimension of truth. This generational shift requires different models and a deeper dimension of truth that results in a higher level of faith. One thing that should distinguish us from former generations is our ability to walk in greater truth. The process we go through may be similar to that of previous generations, but how we navigate that process must be a result of a different paradigm and a higher dimension of truth. Systematic learning is systemic and addresses the whole body to include the systems that govern outcomes in our lives. There is a system behind everything that manifest physically. There is even a system that governs the supernatural dimension of the kingdom. Learning about the kingdom of God leads to adapting a systematic viewpoint on things that manifest in life.

The kingdom of God is a dimensional kingdom having substance and depth that must be sought out and discovered. Holy Spirit as Royal Governor and the Lord Jesus as Lawgiver are assigned to bring us up to the Father's level of truth. You have to seek the kingdom in order to see or be shown another dimension of truth and only someone of greater depth can show you greater dimensions of truth. Dimensional truths are key to entering a kingdom dimension. Dimensional truths challenge foundational beliefs and empower you to come up to the next dimension of truth. Remaining teachable is a key to advancing in the kingdom. Every leader must be connected to someone who can show them another dimension of the truth they already know. If not, we become stuck at a dimension of truth that is not consistent with kingdom truth.

The journey into a greater dimension of kingdom truth began for the disciples in John 1:35-40 when they asked Jesus a simple question. "Rabbi, where do You live?" John the Baptist had already introduced the disciples to the kingdom of God. He had given them an orientation and now they needed someone to lead them into greater kingdom truth. Jesus responded to their inquiry by saying, "come and see." The disciples were seeking the kingdom because they asked the King where He lived. We do not seek what we believe we have already discovered or already have. Many leaders make the mistake of believing they have already discovered the kingdom and therefore do not seek greater kingdom truth. Many have only been introduced to the kingdom and do not walk in greater kingdom truth nor live in a kingdom dimension. I've spent years searching, seeking, researching, and studying the kingdom of God. I've dedicated my life to the learning process of the kingdom in order to possess the kingdom of God and see it manifest in every sphere of my life. It is impossible to overstress the importance of the commitment required in order to enter into and to possess the kingdom of God. The King lives in a kingdom dimension and the kingdom of God is the place where only kings live. From the moment the disciples asked or began to seek, Jesus progressively revealed and demonstrated another dimension of kingdom truth and kingdom living to the disciples. In John 1 the disciples asked the question. In John 2, Jesus turns water into wine. He is answering the disciples question. He is showing them that He lives in a supernatural dimension. Later on, He is asleep on a boat in the midst of a storm. When the disciples awake Him, He again answers the disciples question by exercising dominion over the atmospheric kingdom. Once we are shown another dimension, we have to make a decision to live there and then ask the Royal Governor to bring us up to the level of truth that is required in order to live in that dimension of the kingdom.

This training resource is published to serve the emerging kingdom leaders who are seeking, researching and studying the kingdom of God with a mind to possess the kingdom of God. This is not a book to read but a course to study. For those who are building teaching ministries, teaching bible studies, Sunday School classes, or who may have mentoring and or coaching programs, the course can be used as a train-the-trainer resource. But in order to see the intent of God for this training course fulfilled in your personal life it most important to use the course as a tool that leads you to inquire of Holy Spirit for a greater level of understanding and clarity pertaining to the Father's intent for your life. Never try to understand anything about the kingdom of God without inquiring of Holy Spirit. He is your Master Teacher. The reason the course is entitled, Wise Master Builders Mastery Course, is because the intent is to lead you to ask Holy Spirit the questions you need to ask in order to get the level of understanding required to be successful in building whatever you are appointed to build in the kingdom. I am the author and content developer but not the Master Teacher. John the Baptist pointed the disciples to Jesus, Who would then lead the disciples into a greater dimension of kingdom truth. Jesus finished His assignment and enabled Holy Spirit to return to His original office, function, assignment and role. My assignment as a teacher, trainer, mentor and coach is to set the table for dialog with the Master Teacher, Holy Spirit. Jesus introduced Holy Spirit as our Master Teacher in John 14:26. My style of mentoring and coaching leverages the role of Holy Spirit as Master Teacher, Royal Governor, Leader and Guide. I help with kingdom communications by provoking you to ask Holy Spirit the right questions. Many times our inquiries and questions are off base with the intent of God. Keep in mind the intent of God is the most important thing to God. Holy Spirit wants to stream revelation into our hearts concerning the intent of God. A stream is a consistent flow of revelation and communication. But when we are not asking the right questions, that flow can be interrupted, slow down and even cease, resulting in no response from the home country.

Each lesson in the course is followed by an assessment. The assessment is not a test but is designed to provoke you to process your thoughts on a deeper level and with a different perspective than in the past. The processing of your thoughts on a deeper level will lead to the questions you will then ask Holy Spirit and He will lead you into a kingdom dimension of truth concerning that area of your life.

I am honored to have this opportunity to serve emerging kingdom leaders such as yourself who've decided to receive the grace of God through this training course. My prayer is for you to discover another dimension of the truth you already know leading to an alignment with the intent of God for your life so that you can enter into a kingdom dimension of living. Let Holy Spirit walk you through the process so you too can live where only kings live.

LESSON 1 - KINGDOM MODELS

Mark 10:20, 21 (NKJV)

[20] And he answered and said to Him, "Teacher, all these things I have kept from my youth." [21] Then Jesus, looking at him, loved him, and said to him, "One thing you lack: Go your way, sell whatever you have and give to the poor, and you will have treasure in heaven; and come, take up the cross, and follow Me."

1) The Kingdom of God is the model from which we create kingdom systems to colonize, impact and influence the earth. When Jesus tells the young ruler, "follow Me," He is giving the young man an opportunity to catch a kingdom model, but this young ruler walks away from what was most important to the intent of God for his life. Many times we take what's really important to God for granted because we fail to judge things based on His intent for our lives. The intent of God is not what we want to do nor is it what someone asks us to do. The intent of God is what God has sent us to do and what's most important to God. Holy Spirit will always prioritize the intent of God and we will be faced with decisions to leave or let go of what we want to do and what people are asking us to do in exchange for what God has sent us to do. The essence of Kingdom ruler-ship is understanding how to model kingdom systems and every kingdom system is based on the intent of God. For every emerging kingdom leader, understanding the concept of models and how to model the kingdom of God are very important.

2) Judges 18:1 declares, "In those days there was no king in Israel." Essentially, there was no one who modeled the kingdom of God so the children of Israel were being led into a territory to establish kingdom ruler-ship. This was the intent of God and represents what was most important to Him. The people were going to possess houses and lands but the intent of God was to establish kingdom ruler-ship. We cannot afford to neglect and overlook the intent of God. The Father wants to bless us but it is not His perfect will to do so at the expense of His intent being unfulfilled in the earth. Kingdom citizens must be focused on the intent of God and consider it the most important thing to God. Our entire lives should revolve around the intent of God, what God wants and what is most important to Him.

Philippians 3:17-19 (NKJV)

[17] Brethren, join in following my example, and note those who so walk, as you have us for a pattern. [18] For many walk, of whom I have told you often, and now tell you even

weeping, that they are the enemies of the cross of Christ: [19] whose end is destruction, whose god is their belly, and whose glory is in their shame—who set their mind on earthly things.

3) Models are examples or patterns that can be followed in order to build systems that produce sustainable kingdom results. We must follow kingdom models in order to successfully build whatever we are appointed to build in the kingdom. Our families, marriages, businesses, organizations and ministries, are all based on a system that models something or someone. You cannot produce kingdom results apart from a kingdom model. A primary reason many of our families, marriages, businesses, organizations and ministries do not reflect the reality of the kingdom of God and do not produce consistent tangible kingdom results, is because we have not followed a kingdom model. Our models do not model the kingdom of God. The kingdom of God is an unshakeable kingdom (Hebrews 12:28). While the systems of this world are constantly changing and fading away (1 Corinthians 7:31) the kingdom of God remains constant, consistent and unchangeable. Anything we build that does not model the kingdom of God is subject to fade away, decline and diminish in its ability to impact and influence the quality of life in the earth. When we model the kingdom of God, in spite of everything changing around us, we will continue to be effective and influential through our ministries, businesses, organizations and families.

4) As a result of not having a kingdom model to follow when it came to building the organization God appointed me to build, I spent over 20 years of my life going through a transformation process in order to become the type of organization God intended. Today, what started out as a traditional church model has transformed into the Clarity Training Institute and Leadership Academy where the focus is on teaching, training and equipping emerging kingdom leaders. I believe this organization is on its way to becoming the premiere kingdom leadership training organization in my assigned region. My point in sharing this is to show the impact of not having a kingdom model to follow. The intent of God from the beginning was never a traditional model church but a training organization that was positioned for impact not just in church but in other spheres of society as well. There were no kings in my region who modeled this type of ministry. I didn't have access to anyone who was doing something like this and so by default I followed the same model most follow when they believe they are called to "ministry" and that was a traditional church model.

5) God created Adam as a full grown adult male. Adam was never a baby or an adolescent. Adam never went through a transformation process to become who or what God intended. Adam hit the ground running with the vision of God. We spend years of our lives being transformed in order to become what God intended. Steps in a process can be eliminated by means of having access to kingdom models. There is a great need for kings who model the kingdom of God. Kings are a tangible

expression and representation of the kingdom of God who model the kingdom so others have a reference point for what they are appointed to build.

6) The world tends to understand the concept of models. People like LeBron James have studied and pulled from the models of Michael Jordan and Kobe Bryant. Successful artist in the music industry have studied and pulled from the models of Michael Jackson and Prince. These present day marketplace leaders use the models of their predecessors as a reference point to build their own careers, businesses, organizations and empires. Personally, I've looked at and studied the models of people like Martin Luther King, Jr and John Maxwell. I've also had the opportunity to be mentored by some great leaders who gave me access to their models. Too many leaders try to reinvent the wheel when it comes to building ministries, businesses, organizations and even families. The success and or failures of our predecessors are purposed to be our examples (1 Corinthians 10:6). The intent is (1) we won't fall prey to the same shortcomings and mistakes they made and (2) we would be able to manifest and advance the kingdom of God on a greater level than our predecessors did.

Assessment:

a. Who are you modeling when it comes to prayer, service, family or marriage?

_____

_____

_____

_____

b. We should always consider the outcomes that are being produced by those we follow or model (Hebrews 13:7). Commit some time to studying the model of those you follow or model. Consider the outcomes that are produced. Are these the results you want in your life? Better yet, is this the level of success God has intended for you? Ask Holy Spirit.

_____

_____

_____

_____

c. Never overlook the opportunity to receive from someone who may have some discrepancies in their character or other areas of their life. You simply do not model what you know is not the will of God. A lot of us miss opportunities to gain valuable information because we are looking for a vessel that has no flaws and instead, God sends you to an Eli who has family issues or who does things that do not represent the kingdom of God. Who do you know who does great things but they have issues? What can you learn from them?

_____
_____
_____
_____
_____
_____
_____
_____
_____
_____

LESSON 2 - KINGDOM SYSTEMS

John 2:1-11 (NKJV)

On the third day there was a wedding in Cana of Galilee, and the mother of Jesus was there. ² Now both Jesus and His disciples were invited to the wedding. ³ And when they ran out of wine, the mother of Jesus said to Him, "They have no wine." ⁴ Jesus said to her, "Woman, what does your concern have to do with Me? My hour has not yet come. ⁵ His mother said to the servants, "Whatever He says to you, do it." ⁶ Now there were set there six water pots of stone, according to the manner of purification of the Jews, containing twenty or thirty gallons apiece. ⁷ Jesus said to them, "Fill the water pots with water." And they filled them up to the brim. ⁸ And He said to them, "Draw some out now, and take it to the master of the feast." And they took it. ⁹ When the master of the feast had tasted the water that was made wine, and did not know where it came from (but the servants who had drawn the water knew), the master of the feast called the bridegroom. ¹⁰ And he said to him, "Every man at the beginning sets out the good wine, and when the guests have well drunk, then the inferior. You have kept the good wine until now!"

¹¹ This beginning of signs Jesus did in Cana of Galilee, and manifested His glory; and His disciples believed in Him.

1) Kingdom systems are built based on kingdom models. The significance of systems is the ability to reproduce consistent results. In the parable of the talents, the man who was given one talent hid the talent in the ground (Matthew 25:14-30). When the master calls him to give an account of what he had done the man was rebuked for a lack of productivity and is classified as a lazy and unprofitable servant. The master tells the man he should have at least deposited his money with the bankers. The bankers represent a financial system. The man is rebuked for not taking a systematic approach to increase productivity. A kingdom system is a systematic approach to the will of God with the intent being to reproduce consistent kingdom results.
2) When there is no kingdom system in place there will be no wine. Wine represents provision that manifest supernaturally. In the Jewish wedding, the master of the feast oversaw the order of the wedding including where the guests would be seated and how they would be served. The servants or those appointed to serve, would take

their instructions from the master of the feast. Jesus Mother recognized the limitations of this system because it could not produce wine. Wine again is supernatural provision. At the instruction of His mother, Jesus displaces the master of the feast as the primary leader. The instructions that will govern how provision will flow at the wedding will now come from Jesus and this shift in leadership leads to a shift in an earthly system. Once an earthly system is shifted to the order of a kingdom system, supernatural provision can manifest through that system to produce kingdom results. As kingdom citizens we need to be trained to shift earthly systems just as Jesus did here in order to cause supernatural provision to manifest.

3) Water was essential to the earthly 6 water pot system. Jesus understood how to manage the water that was provided in order to serve the intent of the Father. The intent of the Father was to manifest supernatural provision so that the disciples could see a kingdom system model the Kingdom of God (John 2:11). Two important things happen to set the stage for kingdom results to be produced. (1) Jesus displaces the leader in the earthly system to become the leader who will now govern or give instructions pertaining to how provision will flow. (2) The intent of the Father to demonstrate a kingdom model for the disciples to see was served as a priority through the instructions Jesus gave. Jesus demonstrated His kingdom model to shift earthly systems in order to produce wine or supernatural provision.

Ecclesiastes 9:13-18 (NKJV)

[14] There was a little city with few men in it; and a great king came against it, besieged it, and built great snares around it. [15] Now there was found in it a poor wise man, and he by his wisdom delivered the city. Yet no one remembered that same poor man. [16] Then I said: "Wisdom is better than strength. Nevertheless the poor man's wisdom is despised,
And his words are not heard.

4) The poor wise man had no system by which he could reproduce results. The ability to reproduce results causes you to become known for what you are graced to do and this is how legacies are born. If you can reproduce the results you can also reproduce the rewards associated with that result. Kingdom wealth is tied to the problems you consistently solve. By means of a system that reproduces consistent results, income streams can be created through which you can receive consistent rewards for something you are graced to do. This man wasn't poor because he lacked gifts or grace. This man was poor because he failed to develop a system that could reproduce the results of what he was graced to do.

5) The poor wise man delivered the city by his wisdom which means he did something he was graced to do. But he only did this once which indicates he never developed a system to reproduce that result. We become prominent by means of the problem we consistently solve. Nicodemus told Jesus, we know you come from God because no one can (consistently) do the things you do unless God is with them (John 3:2-3). Jesus turns right around and tells Nicodemus about His model saying "unless you are born again you cannot see (My model) the Kingdom of God. Jesus was graced to do what He did but He also modeled the kingdom of God by means of kingdom systems.

6) Holy Spirit is the CEO of all the affairs of the Kingdom of God in the earth realm. Directions, instructions and guidance must come from Him. The system we are using to manage any form of provision must be shifted to a kingdom system in order to produce sustainable kingdom results. A kingdom system is governed by the leadership of Holy Spirit. In order to shift to a kingdom system (1) you must allow Holy Spirit to fulfill His assignment of being your primary leader, (2) you must receive instructions, directions and guidance from Him. This means you have to consistently ask for His guidance and acknowledge His leadership in your life. (3) You must allow Holy Spirit to align your life, your gifts and your grace with the intent of the Father.

7) The Kingdom of God functions by systems, order, laws, appointment and office. Holy Spirit fills the office of Royal Governor. He is assigned to the earth realm. The Father is seated in Heaven's Celestial Realm which is the highest Kingdom. Jesus Christ is seated at His right hand as High Priest. Holy Spirit is the only Person of the Godhead here in the earth.

8) John 14:16; John 14:26; John 15:26; John 16:7 all use the word "parakletos" which is translated Comforter or Helper when speaking of the role of Holy Spirit. "Parakletos" means to be called to one's side and denotes legal assistant, counsel, advocate, intercessor and comforter which all speak to His office, role and assignment as primary leader in our lives. In His Office, Holy Spirit is the Chief Royal Ambassador and CEO of all of Heaven's affairs in the earth (Genesis 1:1, 2). He is our authority in the earth, who we submit to in the earth and primarily who we communicate with as ambassadors of the Government of God in the earth. No one must ever be allowed to displace His leadership in our lives.

9) Once Adam fell, Holy Spirit had to leave the earth. One of the primary reasons Jesus was manifest in the flesh was to restore the order of the Kingdom that had been disrupted by the enemy (1 John 3:8). Holy Spirit had to return to His original office, role and assignment. Jesus talks about this in John 16:7 when He says "if I do not go away the Helper will not come to you. But if I depart I will send Him to you." In John 20:17, Jesus said, "do not touch or cling, which means to attach yourself, to Me." On the other hand, Holy Spirit is revealed as "Parakletos" in earlier chapters of John's gospel. Parakletos is where we get the word parasite. Many people cling to the

revelation of Jesus manifest in the earth. They don't know the risen King in His Office as High Priest. They continue to ask the "Lord to lead and guide" when Holy Spirit is assigned to fulfill this role in their lives. Holy Spirit is the One we should cling to for guidance and direction. As long as Jesus was in the earth, He was in the Office of Holy Spirit. Jesus had to leave in order for Holy Spirit to return to His original Office, function, role and assignment.
10) The impact we have in the earth will be in direct proportion to our understanding and submission to the leadership of Holy Spirit. The role of Holy Spirit parallels that of Jesus when He walked the earth (John 16:5-15). This is a very important concept because this means we do not interact with Jesus in the same way as the original disciples interacted with Him. We must now interact with Holy Spirit in the same way the original disciples interacted with Jesus.

1 Kings 17:8-16 (NKJV)

[8] Then the word of the LORD came to him, saying, [9] "Arise, go to Zarephath, which belongs to Sidon, and dwell there. See, I have commanded a widow there to provide for you." [10] So he arose and went to Zarephath. And when he came to the gate of the city, indeed a widow was there gathering sticks. And he called to her and said, "Please bring me a little water in a cup, that I may drink." [11] And as she was going to get it, he called to her and said, "Please bring me a morsel of bread in your hand."

[12] So she said, "As the LORD your God lives, I do not have bread, only a handful of flour in a bin, and a little oil in a jar; and see, I am gathering a couple of sticks that I may go in and prepare it for myself and my son, that we may eat it, and die."

[13] And Elijah said to her, "Do not fear; go and do as you have said, but make me a small cake from it first, and bring it to me; and afterward make some for yourself and your son. [14] For thus says the LORD God of Israel: 'The bin of flour shall not be used up, nor shall the jar of oil run dry, until the day the LORD sends rain on the earth.'"

[15] So she went away and did according to the word of Elijah; and she and he and her household ate for many days. [16] The bin of flour was not used up, nor did the jar of oil run dry, according to the word of the LORD which He spoke by Elijah.

11) Every system has something that is essential to that system. Oil and flour were essential to the widows system that governed how she managed her provision. In the

Old Testament the prophet represents the intent of God. In order to shift to a kingdom system Elijah must be served first because the intent of God is essential to any kingdom system. Order is set in a system by means of what is set or appointed first. Everything else follows the order of what is set first. Elijah asks the widow to make him a cake first because the intent of God must always be served first in any kingdom system. As long as our own needs are the priority we are not operating in a kingdom system. Once the intent of God is accommodated in the proper order in her system, the widow's earthly system for managing provision is shifted to a kingdom system through which the Kingdom of God could manifest supernatural increase.

12) There is a kingdom system behind the manifestation of supernatural provision. Once we shift to a kingdom system that governs how we manage provision, we can expect provision to manifest supernaturally consistently. The supernatural dimension is not just something God does when He feels like it. The kingdom of God is a supernatural kingdom governed by laws and principles through which a physical reality that reflects the kingdom of heaven can manifest here on earth.

2 Kings 6:1-7 (NKJV)

6 And the sons of the prophets said to Elisha, "See now, the place where we dwell with you is too small for us. ² Please, let us go to the Jordan, and let every man take a beam from there, and let us make there a place where we may dwell." So he answered, "Go." ³ Then one said, "Please consent to go with your servants." And he answered, "I will go." ⁴ So he went with them. And when they came to the Jordan, they cut down trees. ⁵ But as one was cutting down a tree, the iron ax head fell into the water; and he cried out and said, "Alas, master! For it was borrowed."

⁶ So the man of God said, "Where did it fall?" And he showed him the place. So he cut off a stick, and threw it in there; and he made the iron float. ⁷ Therefore he said, "Pick it up for yourself." So he reached out his hand and took it.

13) Water, air, fire, wood, and metal are essential elements to the earth's system. When you place wood in water, the essential elements in the wood cause the water system to shift enabling the wood to float. When you put water in fire the essential elements in the water causes the fire to shift and the fire goes out. Put metal in fire and the essential elements in the fire cause a shift in the metal and the metal breaks down. Air in our bodies enables our bodies to float on water. Elisha put a stick or wood in

the water to cause a shift in the water and the iron axe head floated. Elisha understood the systematic makeup of the earth's system and as a result he also understood how to shift earthly systems. Supernatural manifestation is governed by a kingdom system.

Assessment:

a. Systems have the ability to reproduce results. Look at specific areas of your life where you are experiencing a level of success and things are flowing. What are you doing systematically that contributes to the success in this area of your life?

_____
_____
_____
_____
_____
_____
_____

b. There is a science to every system. The science is the stratagem behind winning. Stratagem is a plan or scheme used to outwit an opponent or to achieve an end. Intangibles are a key to a winning stratagem. Some examples of intangibles are consistency, endurance, and tenacity. What intangibles do you believe are your strengths? What intangibles do you need to develop in order to support a winning stratagem?

_____
_____
_____
_____
_____
_____

c. Life is lived daily. A system that produces a high level of productivity in the will of God on a daily basis is essential to winning in life and fulfilling the intent of God. Describe your system for productivity on a daily basis. Begin with your system for getting the proper rest and managing your energy and include how you manage your time.

d. What nonproductive activities are draining your energy and contributing to broken focus? What adjustments do you need to make to remove stress from your life and bring your life into alignment with the will of God to be more productive in what He has appointed for you?

LESSON 3 - LEGAL REQUIREMENTS

Matthew 3:13-16 (NKJV)

¹³ Then Jesus came from Galilee to John at the Jordan to be baptized by him. ¹⁴ And John tried to prevent Him, saying, "I need to be baptized by You, and are You coming to me?" ¹⁵ But Jesus answered and said to him, "Permit it to be so now, for thus it is fitting for us to fulfill all righteousness." Then he allowed Him.

¹⁶ When He had been baptized, Jesus came up immediately from the water; and behold, the heavens were opened to Him, and He saw the Spirit of God descending like a dove and alighting upon Him.

1) The heavens were opened once Jesus fulfilled all righteousness. Open heavens represent a supernatural dimension where supernatural manifestation is governed by a kingdom system. Righteousness is a legal term and represents the legal requirements of and alignment with the intent of God. In order to create kingdom life systems that enable us to live in a supernatural dimension, we have to fulfill all righteousness or satisfy all of the legal requirements of righteousness. This explains why we are instructed to seek first the kingdom of God and His righteousness (Matthew 6:33). Essentially, this means we are seeking to be in agreement and alignment with the intent and the will of God for whatever area of life we want to see the kingdom of God manifest.

2) The kingdom of God is a realignment with the intent of God for my life. Many of us assume we are in agreement with the intent of God as a result of experiencing some good results. I chose a career in the computer field in which I worked for over 20 years. At some point in my life Holy Spirit began to lead me away from that career path. I struggled with this leading because I had done well financially in this career. One day Holy Spirit said to me, Rodney, computers are what you chose but it was never the intent of God for your life. The Father has just been using that for your provision all these years. Perhaps the Father has been using something that is not His intent or perfect will for your life too. Kingdom results will only be produced by means of agreement and alignment with the intent of God. Although we may have done well doing some things, this is no indication that these things represent the intent of God for our lives. You cannot operate on assumptions when it comes to the will and the intent of God. You must see clearly into the intent of God by means of the leadership of Holy Spirit.

3) "Jesus came from Galilee to John at the Jordan to be baptized by him." These are simple instructions yet they are legal requirements. Whenever we overlook small details of the instructions we are given we compromise supernatural manifestation because we haven't met all of the legal requirements. The legal requirements for accessing a kingdom dimension are always based on the intent of God. It is illegal for the Kingdom of God to manifest outside of the intent of God. Jesus had to leave Galilee, go to John at the Jordan and then execute the will of the Father to be baptized by John at the Jordan. All righteousness was fulfilled only after Jesus executed each of these instructions. The intent of God is not (1) what you've chosen to do or (2) what someone has asked you to do. The intent of God is (1) what God requires of you, (2) what God has sent you to do and (3) God's why for anything He does for you.

Hebrews 10:35-38 (NKJV)

[35] Therefore do not cast away your confidence, which has great reward. [36] For you have need of endurance, so that after you have done the will of God, you may receive the promise: [37] "For yet a little while, And He who is coming will come and will not tarry. [38] Now the just shall live by faith; But if anyone draws back, My soul has no pleasure in him."

5) Enduring the process of the will of God to get into a receive position is also a legal requirement. After we complete the process of the will of God we may receive the promise. Notice the use of the word "may" in this scripture. The word "may" is for those who hate process and try to force the hand of God through some other means other than executing the instructions of the will of God. The word "may" indicates this is a requirement and if we do not complete the process of the will of God we "may" not receive the promise. You will be amazed at what is required by the process of the will of God. A lot of what God requires of us will serve to prove our motives and our willingness to remain submitted to the leadership of Holy Spirit. When we kick against the prick we frustrate the grace of God and miss an opportunity to experience a supernatural dimension of kingdom living.

2 Corinthians 5:7 (NKJV)

[7] For we walk by faith, not by sight.

6) Faith is a not a choice but also a legal requirement. Kingdom faith is a process that adjusts our truth to agree with God's truth in order to bring us to a place where we

see what God sees. To be informed can sometimes be a violation of the legal requirement of faith. Holy Spirit therefore does not inform us how manifestation will come because this would violate faith. Holy Spirit leads us and conforms us (Romans 8:29). Seeing what God sees is a legal requirement. Get comfortable with being conformed while not being informed.

7) Truth is dimensional and Holy Spirit is appointed to lead us into all truth, greater truth, higher dimensions of truth and kingdom truth (John 16:13). There is another dimension to the truth we know. Holy Spirit wants to bring us up to the next dimension of truth. Jesus prayed for us that we would be brought up to His level of truth so that we could have the same level of relationship with the Father as He has (John 17:11-26). Fellowship with the Father is for those who have been perfected in the concepts and principles that pertain to who the Father is. We must see the Father as He is in order to have true fellowship with Him (Hebrews 11:6). If we say we have fellowship with Him and there is darkness in us, we lie and do not practice the truth (1 John 1:6).

8) A key to the next dimension of truth is to remain teachable. Whenever our current dimension of truth is challenged, the intent is to pull us up to the next dimension of truth or to greater kingdom truth. Do not harden your heart when your current level of truth is being challenged (Hebrews 4:7-10). You have to remain teachable in order to enter His rest. Being teachable means you willingly subject everything you know to the truth that is currently being revealed. You remain pliable and recognize when greater truth steps into the room (Luke 5:1-9).

Assessment:

a. List some things you believe God has promised you or some things you believe should have happened for you by now. What are some things Holy Spirit has been leading you to do that you've not yet fully executed? What currencies or resources have you committed to what Holy Spirit has been leading you to do?

_____

_____

_____

_____

_____

_____

b. What is the Father's intent for doing what He has promised you? What does He want out of it? If you do not know ask Holy Spirit. This is essential to the fulfillment of the promise.

c. A promise without a principle will not come to pass. Overlooking the small details of an instruction can become a major obstacle to the promise being fulfilled. What we see as a small insignificant detail is a big thing to God because every transaction the kingdom of heaven makes in the earth realm must be a legal transaction. Ask Holy Spirit what have you missed, overlooked or failed to execute resulting in the promise not yet being fulfilled.

LESSON 4 - DREAMERS AND VISIONARIES

Ephesians 5:8-17 (NKJV)

⁸ For you were once darkness, but now you are light in the Lord. Walk as children of light ⁹ (for the fruit of the Spirit is in all goodness, righteousness, and truth), ¹⁰ finding out what is acceptable to the Lord. ¹¹ And have no fellowship with the unfruitful works of darkness, but rather expose them. ¹² For it is shameful even to speak of those things which are done by them in secret. ¹³ But all things that are [c]exposed are made manifest by the light, for whatever makes manifest is light. ¹⁴ Therefore He says:

"Awake, you who sleep, Arise from the dead,
And Christ will give you light." ¹⁵ See then that you walk circumspectly, not as fools but as wise, ¹⁶ redeeming the time, because the days are evil. ¹⁷ Therefore do not be unwise, but understand what the will of the Lord is.

1) A dream is ours but a vision is from God. Dreams include many things we just want to do that are also things God never appointed or sent us to do. Our dreams therefore must be reconciled with God's vision. Being a dreamer will lead you into many unfruitful things that are not inspired by the will of God. Ephesians 5 calls these things the unfruitful works of darkness. Unfruitful works of darkness are a primary reason many never discover the intent and purpose of God for their lives. Too many are preoccupied by things that have no relevance to the intent of God for their lives. Unfruitful works of darkness detain us from the discovery of the will of God by means of occupying space and keeping us busy with a lot of meaningless and unfruitful activities and events. At a certain point in my life, Holy Spirit led me to evaluate and assess what was really working and what was not. At that time I was doing a lot of things to include traveling to Africa and other areas outside of my assigned region for missions and meetings. But at the end of the day I could not see any real fruit from all I was doing. I stopped and sat still long enough to get clarity on the will of God for my life. This enabled me to see the effect of unfruitful works of darkness on my life. Essentially, I wasted a lot of time on things that were not important because they had no relevance as far as the intent of God for my life was concerned.

2) God operates by appointment and nothing should be added or taken away from what He has appointed (Ecclesiastes 3:14). Anything God has not appointed will be a deterrent to what you are appointed and sent to do. One of the best decisions I

ever made was to stop doing what I was being asked to do in order to sit still long enough to discover what I was sent to do. After years of being frustrated with not seeing kingdom results, I made a decision to cut off unfruitful works of darkness and almost immediately I began to receive light. Light is the sound of the will of God and the frequency of the Father's communication. I sat still for a period of 2-3 years and listened intently to Holy Spirit as He gave me greater clarity and understanding on the purpose and intent of God for my life.

3) Dreamers are asleep which means they are more in tune to darkness than light. Ephesians 5 issues a wakeup call. We don't realize we've been asleep until we wake up and no one really likes the sound of the alarm. The sound of the will of God may come in the form of some disturbing news that reveals a problem you've been sent to solve. Most of what we are involved in while asleep are things we want to do, like to do or have been asked to do by someone other than God. These unfruitful works of darkness have kept you away from the will of God long enough. Something is missing from your life because you are missing from the will of God. Don't spend your life dreaming! It's time to wake up!

1 Corinthians 13:11, 12 (NKJV)

¹¹ When I was a child, I spoke as a child, I understood as a child, I thought as a child; but when I became a man, I put away childish things. ¹² For now we see in a mirror, dimly, but then face to face. Now I know in part, but then I shall know just as I also am known.

4) As a kid I dreamed of playing professional basketball. What is interesting is that I would often dream about basketball as I was searching for a purpose in life. As I matured and began to get greater clarity on the Father's intent for my life, I realized the basketball dreams were occupying space in my heart in the place of God's vision for my life. I also realized I was called to do something great that had nothing to do with basketball. Basketball was only a childhood dream in my subconscious mind. Childhood dreams may serve as placeholders for the vision of God but they can also cause misinterpretations of God given dreams. Once I received greater clarity and understanding pertaining to the intent and purpose of God for my life, I realized what I had been dreaming about all my adult life was what God had sent me to do but because I couldn't specifically identify what that was, Holy Spirit used basketball to represent the Fathers' vision for my life. Recently, one of my childhood all-time favorite basketball players died. His passing was a prophetic sign to me that my childhood dream had also now died. I was no longer chasing someone else's dream. You see it was not just the childhood dream of basketball that occupied space in my heart, but there were other things I dreamed of doing because I saw someone else doing those things. But once I understood the original intent of God for my own

life, my dreams were reconciled with God's vision for my life. During the time of this former basketball player's passing, Holy Spirit said to me, "now I can speak to you clearly about the Father's vision for your life."
5) We tend to interpret God given dreams based on our own dreams. Our dreams therefore can distort the revelation of what Holy Spirit is really saying to us in a God given dream. As we mature, we put away childish dreams and come to a reality of what Holy Spirit is really saying to us in our dreams. God's vision can now be shaped and formed in our heart as a result our dreams being reconciled with His vision for our life.

<u>Assessment:</u>

a. What are your reoccurring dreams? How long have you had these dreams? A dream that reoccurs many times is an indication that we've misinterpreted what Holy Spirit is revealing and we've not yet really understood what He is saying. Ask Holy Spirit what He is saying through these reoccurring dreams.

_____
_____
_____
_____
_____
_____
_____
_____
_____
_____

b. The similitude that appears in God given dreams are the signs and symbols of high level kingdom communications (Hosea 12:10). What signs and symbols consistently show up in your dreams? What do these people and or things mean to you? These signs and symbols are essential components to your dream language. Once you can interpret a sign or symbol, the meaning will be consistent in every dream. Before you purchase that book on interpreting dreams, ask Holy Spirit to help you interpret your dream language. He might just lead you to that book on interpreting dreams or He might lead you in a completely different way. The point here is by asking you are submitting to His leadership.

c. Compare your interpretation of your dreams to what Holy Spirit has been communicating. Has there been any movement or fruit based on your interpretation? If not, it is time to ask Holy Spirit what He is really saying through these dreams. Make sure you are not misinterpreting God given dreams by means of your own childhood dreams.

d. The intent of God is not what you want to do nor is it what people are asking you to do. The intent of God is what you've been sent to do. What types of opportunities are consistently presented to you? How have you responded? Have you ignored these opportunities in order to pursue something else you want or like to do?

_____
_____
_____
_____
_____
_____
_____
_____
_____
_____
_____
_____
_____

LESSON 5 - EMERGING KINGDOM LEADERS

Luke 12:35-48 (NKJV)

35 "Let your waist be girded and your lamps burning; 36 and you yourselves be like men who wait for their master, when he will return from the wedding, that when he comes and knocks they may open to him immediately. 37 Blessed are those servants whom the master, when he comes, will find watching. Assuredly, I say to you that he will gird himself and have them sit down to eat, and will come and serve them. 38 And if he should come in the second watch, or come in the third watch, and find them so, blessed are those servants. 39 But know this, that if the master of the house had known what hour the thief would come, he would [a]have watched and not allowed his house to be broken into. 40 Therefore you also be ready, for the Son of Man is coming at an hour you do not expect."

41 Then Peter said to Him, "Lord, do You speak this parable only to us, or to all people?"

42 And the Lord said, "Who then is that faithful and wise steward, whom his master will make ruler over his household, to give them their portion of food in due season? 43 Blessed is that servant whom his master will find so doing when he comes. 44 Truly, I say to you that he will make him ruler over all that he has. 45 But if that servant says in his heart, 'My master is delaying his coming,' and begins to beat the male and female servants, and to eat and drink and be drunk, 46 the master of that servant will come on a day when he is not looking for him, and at an hour when he is not aware, and will cut him in two and appoint him his portion with the unbelievers. 47 And that servant who knew his master's will, and did not prepare himself or do according to his will, shall be beaten with many stripes. 48 But he who did not know, yet committed things deserving of stripes, shall be beaten with few. For everyone to whom much is given, from him much will be required; and to whom much has been committed, of him they will ask the more.

1) The vision God has for your life comes down to a plan to serve the body of Christ and or the population at large with whatever dimension of grace and anointing He has freely given to you. In the movie Black Panther, the former regime of leaders create a problem for the current regime as a result of not having a vision to serve the population at large with a resource that had been freely given to them. This resource

had the potential to change the quality of life for the entire world but instead of sharing, they hid and kept this to themselves to serve only their own needs and personal agenda. This approach caused the current leadership to come under attack. Whenever leadership lacks a vision to serve beyond our own personal and internal needs, we violate the intent of God resulting in those we are appointed to serve eventually turning on us.

2) Any problem we are sent to solve but that we consistently overlook and ignore, that same problem will eventually visit our house. This should lead us to look at how many in our families, organizations or ministries have family members who are incarcerated, abused, addicted, mentally ill, live in poverty, are homeless or jobless. There is no coincidence that these social issues are somehow connected to us. As leaders, we must have a vision to serve the intent of God first. When we are wise and faithful over what God has given us, the Kingdom of God appoints those who will serve us. Jesus said He would come and sit down to serve us. Whenever we fail to show up to serve the intent of God, something or someone who is appointed to serve us does not show up for us. Blessed is the servant who is found doing what they are appointed to do and serving the intent of God through that service. Those who have a vision to serve the body of Christ and the population at large and who appropriate what has been freely given to them in this service, are the emerging kingdom leaders of today. These leaders are coming out of hiding or places of captivity to rule, lead and be king (Ecclesiastes 4:13, 14).

Matthew 8:8, 9 (NKJV)

⁸ The centurion answered and said, "Lord, I am not worthy that You should come under my roof. But only speak a word, and my servant will be healed. ⁹ For I also am a man under authority, having soldiers under me. And I say to this one, 'Go,' and he goes; and to another, 'Come,' and he comes; and to my servant, 'Do this,' and he does it."

3) The centurion was an effective leader because he understood authority, the law of submission and how to be led. Understanding (1) the principle of submission (2) how to receive and follow instruction and (3) how to be led are essential to effective leadership in the kingdom of God. The basis for kingdom leadership is self-mastery that results in being submitted to the leadership of Holy Spirit in each subdomain of the human kingdom (1 Timothy 3:1-12). Gifts are never the basis for kingdom leadership. Many gifted, anointed, charismatic, educated and intelligent people are not effective when it comes to leadership because of a failure to balance gifts with intangibles such as love, faith, hope, patience, endurance, consistency, and discipline. When we neglect to develop these types of intangibles we become messy in our service. The kingdom of God is a call to a higher level of service. This high level

service is reflected in a level of professionalism and high class service. One of the most enjoyable experiences is to be served by someone who provides a high level of service based on their gifts and grace. Effective leadership is essential to the fulfillment of the purpose and intent of God in the earth.

4) Effective kingdom leadership begins with understanding Holy Spirit, His office, function, role and assignment and submission to His leadership in every area of your life. As emerging kingdom leaders, before we will be able to successfully advance the kingdom of God effectively in a territory or sphere such as business, education, media, arts and entertainment or government we must learn to apply the law of submission in life and to follow the lead of Holy Spirit.

5) The primary agenda of Satan has always been to displace the leadership of Holy Spirit in our lives. Satan's primary target in your life is not your faith, your anointing, your family, your money or your health. The devil wants to influence leadership in your life by means of displacing the leadership of God in your life. If he can influence the leadership of your life he can introduce death, destruction and all manner of evil into any area of your life. Once the leadership of God is displaced, any model of leadership we embrace becomes problematic because that model of leadership is subject to be influenced by the enemy through the will of man, humanistic wisdom or secular humanism.

1 Samuel 8:11-20 (NKJV)

[11] And he said, "This will be the behavior of the king who will reign over you: He will take your sons and appoint them for his own chariots and to be his horsemen, and some will run before his chariots. [12] He will appoint captains over his thousands and captains over his fifties, will set some to plow his ground and reap his harvest, and some to make his weapons of war and equipment for his chariots. [13] He will take your daughters to be perfumers, cooks, and bakers. [14] And he will take the best of your fields, your vineyards, and your olive groves, and give them to his servants. [15] He will take a tenth of your grain and your vintage, and give it to his officers and servants. [16] And he will take your male servants, your female servants, your finest [a]young men, and your donkeys, and put them to his work. [17] He will take a tenth of your sheep. And you will be his servants. [18] And you will cry out in that day because of your king whom you have chosen for yourselves, and the LORD will not hear you in that day."

[19] Nevertheless the people refused to obey the voice of Samuel; and they said, "No, but we will have a king over us, [20] that we also may be like all the nations, and that our king may judge us and go out before us and fight our battles."

6) The history of leadership bears witness to the attempt of the enemy to displace the leadership of God. In 1 Samuel 8, the people of God demand a king because they wanted to be like the other nations who were under Babylonian ruler-ship. They effectively reject the leadership of God and embrace a model of leadership God never intended for them. It was always the intent of God to be primary leader in our lives through the person of Holy Spirit. Keep in mind, the people who were demanding a king were under the influence of a Babylonian mindset. The objective of the Babylonian mindset is independence from God because this mindset is influenced by Satan himself. Five-fold ministry gifts and other grace gift leaders have their place and a role to play in our lives but there is a space in our lives reserved only for God. Whenever we allow anyone in the space reserved for God, we violate the law of space and prove our loyalty to those we've allowed to occupy that space. The problem is in so doing we disprove our loyalty to God specifically in the area of submitting to the leadership of Holy Spirit. Take note of what Samuel said would happen once the people embraced a form of leadership God never intended. Pay particular attention to what Samuel said would be the behavior of this king. Everything he does will serve his own interests and agenda. In other words, this model of leadership is based on the will of man. The problem being the will of man can be influenced by the enemy. Many are following this model of leadership today where the intent of God is not served and is certainly not the priority. This model of leadership is based on a fallen paradigm and the church will never fulfill a divine purpose if we continue to follow this model.

1 Timothy 3:1-7 (NKJV)

3 This is a faithful saying: If a man desires the position of a bishop, he desires a good work. [2] A bishop then must be blameless, the husband of one wife, temperate, sober-minded, of good behavior, hospitable, able to teach; [3] not given to wine, not violent, not greedy for money, but gentle, not quarrelsome, not covetous; [4] one who rules his own house well, having his children in submission with all reverence [5] (for if a man does not know how to rule his own house, how will he take care of the church of God?); [6] not a novice, lest being puffed up with pride he fall into the same condemnation as the devil. [7] Moreover he

must have a good testimony among those who are outside, lest he fall into reproach and the snare of the devil.

7) The basis for kingdom leadership is self-mastery or the ability "rule his own house well." This concept becomes clear once we look at a model that subdivides our lives into 5 basic subdomains of the human kingdom. Self-mastery is the ability to submit an area of my life to the Lordship of Christ. Whatever we fail to master in life will master us (1 Corinthians 6:12; 2 Peter 2:19). Going through the process of bringing the subdomains of our human kingdom into alignment with the kingdom of God prepares us to be a leader in advancing the kingdom of God effectively in an external territory or sphere.

8) In order to align our lives with the intent of God so that the will of God can flow freely through our lives, each of these subdomains must be submitted to the Lordship of Christ and then governed by Holy Spirit. Each of these subdomains, if not managed properly, has the potential to interrupt and restrict the flow of the will of God in and through our lives. Management of the 5 subdomains will be virtually impossible apart from self-mastery. The inability or unwillingness to submit to the Lordship of Christ means our lives will not be governed by Holy Spirit.

9) Holy Spirit governs any area of our lives that we fully submit to the Lordship of Christ. We lack detailed instructions, direction and guidance from Holy Spirit in any area of life that is not fully submitted to the Lordship of Christ. Chaotic, disorderly

and areas of our lives that do not reflect the reality of the Kingdom of God are an indication that we've not fully submitted those areas of our lives to the Lordship of Jesus Christ and therefore Holy Spirit is not governing those areas of our lives. Once Holy Spirit begins to govern an area of our lives, transformation takes place and the landscape of that area of life begins to shift and change in order to reflect the reality of the Kingdom of God. Remain submitted to and be patient with this process. Results are imminent.

10) Lordship is jurisdictional and any area we have not truly submitted to the Lordship of Christ will be out of the jurisdiction of Holy Spirit to give detailed instruction, direction and guidance. Many times we receive a "word" from the Lord and then run off in an attempt to execute that word on our own. Once we fail to get the intended results we return to Holy Spirit for help. This is not the will of God for sons of God. Sons of God never detach from the leadership of Holy Spirit. We consistently ask for direction and guidance throughout the course of the day. Sons of God understand the Father is not impressed and does not bless anything we attempt to do in our own strength (Psalm 147:10).

Assessment:

a. The chart on the previous page is a great tool that can be used to evaluate and bring alignment to the subdomains of your life. Study the chart carefully and then evaluate each subdomain of your life. Give yourself a score on a scale of 1-5 with 5 being the highest. To score a 5 would indicate the will of God is flowing freely in that area of your life and you are seeing kingdom results manifest.

_____

_____

_____

_____

_____

_____

_____

b. To what do you attribute your high scores? What about the low scores?

_____
_____
_____
_____
_____
_____
_____
_____

c. Look again at the subdomains where you've scored the highest and ask Holy Spirit if the decisions you've made in these areas are restricting the will of God in another subdomain of your life.

_____
_____
_____
_____
_____
_____
_____
_____

d. In order to differentiate your own choices from the intent and will of God, ask Holy Spirit to help you classify the decisions you've made about career, ministry, family, business and relationships. Is there something God has used but it's not really His perfect will for your life?

_____
_____
_____
_____
_____
_____
_____
_____
_____
_____

e. Meditate on Mark 10:23-31. What areas of your life will have to be reconstructed in order to align with the kingdom of God? How do you feel about starting over in this area of your life?

_____
_____
_____
_____
_____
_____
_____
_____
_____
_____

f. The idea of starting over can be overwhelming once we consider what it has taken to get to where we are in that area of life. This is where courage and tenacity come into play. The violent possess the kingdom by force. You will reach a destination a lot quicker when you understand how to be led by the Royal Governor. Make a commitment to totally depend on His leadership and communicate this to Him in prayer.

_____

_____

_____

_____

_____

_____

_____

_____

_____

_____

_____

LESSON 6 - SMALL VISION – SMALL PROVISION

Matthew 6:25-34 (NKJV)

²⁵ "Therefore I say to you, do not worry about your life, what you will eat or what you will drink; nor about your body, what you will put on. Is not life more than food and the body more than clothing? ²⁶ Look at the birds of the air, for they neither sow nor reap nor gather into barns; yet your heavenly Father feeds them. Are you not of more value than they? ²⁷ Which of you by worrying can add one cubit to his stature?

²⁸ "So why do you worry about clothing? Consider the lilies of the field, how they grow: they neither toil nor spin; ²⁹ and yet I say to you that even Solomon in all his glory was not [c]arrayed like one of these. ³⁰ Now if God so clothes the grass of the field, which today is, and tomorrow is thrown into the oven, will He not much more clothe you, O you of little faith?

³¹ "Therefore do not worry, saying, 'What shall we eat?' or 'What shall we drink?' or 'What shall we wear?' ³² For after all these things the Gentiles seek. For your heavenly Father knows that you need all these things. ³³ But seek first the kingdom of God and His righteousness, and all these things shall be added to you.³⁴ Therefore do not worry about tomorrow, for tomorrow will worry about its own things. Sufficient for the day is its own trouble.

1) Natural or physical manifestation follows and is a result of our spiritual position and condition. If something is missing or coming up short in my physical realm this is a reflection of something missing or coming up short as it pertains to the will or intent of God in my spiritual realm. If provision consistently shows up small this indicates that I have small vision for my life. Small vision is a result of focusing only on your own provision. Small means limited; of little consequence and of minor influence. Provision that only meets my own need is small. To some this may sound ungrateful. But you have to understand the intent of God is for you to have massive impact in the earth. Just having your own needs met does not facilitate this level of impact or influence.
2) Many of us think small and have small vision for our lives. Small vision is really just a dream. A dream is ours but a vision is from God. Mary dreamed of getting married

but God had a vision that she would give birth to the Savior of the world. God's vision for our lives is so much greater than our own dreams. God only has vision for generations. He has always been focused on generations. He is the God of Abraham, Isaac and Jacob. Until your vision becomes generational, your vision is just a dream and too small to serve the intent of God.

3) There are capacity requirements to the will of God and it is a violation to do something on a lesser level than God intended. God does not bless what we can do in our own strength (Psalm 147:10,11). The truth is that we can do good in and of ourselves. In order to move into a dimension that is pleasing to God, we have to tap into the grace of God. We are God-class hybrid beings. We are part god and part human. When Jesus spoke to and exercised dominion over the atmospheric kingdom, the disciples asked, "who can this be," or in other words what kind of man is this," (Mark 4:39-41). The disciples were seeing a God-man, hybrid being exercise dominion over the atmospheric kingdom. Jesus is our prototypical leader. He is the model we are to follow and pattern ourselves after as sons of God. Holy Spirit is assigned to show us how to do this.

4) It's the God side that we need to understand how to activate and tap into. The God side of us starts with our gifts and grace. Anything we are doing that does not utilize the gifts and grace God has invested in us will never exceed being just good because we are only utilizing our own strength, intellect, skills and natural abilities. Our gifts are a primary means of access to the grace of God. Gifts and grace work together which is why the two are sometimes referred to as gift grace. Our gifts and grace should become so integrated in our lives to the point we are not able to recognize where we end and God begins or where God begins and we end. Apostle Paul said it this way in 2 Corinthians 12:2. "I know a man in Christ who fourteen years ago whether in the body I do not know, or whether out of the body I do not know, God knows such a one was caught up to the third heaven. Paul's gifts and grace were so integrated in his life that seeing, hearing and knowing spiritual truths came natural to him. Paul was in touch with his God nature or divine nature. This is how we maximize our gifts and grace.

1 Samuel 17:50-54 (NKJV)

[50] So David prevailed over the Philistine with a sling and a stone, and struck the Philistine and killed him. But there was no sword in the hand of David. [51] Therefore David ran and stood over the Philistine, took his sword and drew it out of its sheath and killed him, and cut off his head with it.

And when the Philistines saw that their champion was dead, they fled. ⁵² Now the men of Israel and Judah arose and shouted, and pursued the Philistines as far as the entrance of [a]the valley and to the gates of Ekron. And the wounded of the Philistines fell along the road to Shaaraim, even as far as Gath and Ekron. ⁵³ Then the children of Israel returned from chasing the Philistines, and they plundered their tents. ⁵⁴ And David took the head of the Philistine and brought it to Jerusalem, but he put his armor in his tent.

4) Many of us settle for just having needs met and never set goals beyond that. Goals should not be limited to needs. Our goals should challenge the Goliath's in our life. Goliath represents (1) your greatest challenge contributing to smallness in your life and (2) your greatest breakthrough. If you can defeat the Goliath in your life, you can experience your greatest breakthrough. As a God class hybrid being, we are equipped for greatness. Everyone, including ourselves deserve better from us. Many of us settle for good in life and we often speak of the goodness of the Lord. We even have clichés that emphasize a good dimension of the will of God. Keep in mind that good is something we can accomplish on our own. But then there is an acceptable and perfect dimension of the will of God that requires the gifts and grace God has invested in us (Romans 12:2). It is not the intent of God for us to just do good in life. Set goals that stretch beyond good to the acceptable and even the perfect will of God. If God didn't want you to have this dimension of His will in your life, He would have never declared this in His word.

5) When David used the sling shot and stone to bring Goliath down, he was led to target Goliath's head. The head represents the operations center or place where important decisions are made. The head also represents what was essential to the system that Goliath represents. A primary key to breaking the limitation of smallness is to displace small thinking by means of shifting to a system where Holy Spirit governs our subconscious realm. The subconscious realm is the subdomain that houses our thoughts and our decision making process. You are being led by whoever or whatever has the greatest influence on your thinking, your thoughts and your decisions. The mind of Christ must be the epicenter of all our operations. We have to submit our subconscious realm to the Lordship of Christ so that Holy Spirit can govern or influence our thinking, our thoughts and our decisions.

6) Goliath's head became David's trophy because this was a major breakthrough. Goliath or the system he represents was behind the small thinking of the people he challenged. This system held the people of God captive and immobilized them from advancing or moving forward. Goliath marked his territory and defied anyone to step beyond those boundaries. What most people do not realize is there is a system behind the limitation of smallness in our lives. This system holds us captive by means of influencing our thinking, our thoughts and our decisions. In order to break

through the barrier of this limitation we have to unplug this system and get plugged into a kingdom system where Holy Spirit has the greatest influence on our thinking, our thoughts and our decisions.

7) Once Goliath is defeated the entire army of Israel advances. The captives are set free and can now see themselves living beyond the previous limitations. Everyone under Saul's command was influenced by his limited thinking. Saul was afraid of Goliath. Fear is simply a form of limited thinking. David was not under Saul's influence because he had been given what may have appeared to be the less notable task of taking care of the sheep. This separation from Saul was intentional. God did not want David to be influenced by Saul. Everyone will not embrace a kingdom dimension. Many will simply not want to go through the process of paying the price for what it takes to enter into a kingdom dimension of life. Goliath was a champion because no one challenged his system, that is until David showed up. Those who are courageous enough to challenge the systems of this world can become champions for the kingdom of God. The influence of one champion will impact the lives of many. David is another prototypical leader who gives us a kingdom model to follow. David's model show us how to devise a kingdom system to challenge the systems of this world that impact and influence the quality of life we live here on earth.

8) The systems of this world influence us to focus only on our own provision and this creates small vision for our lives. Small vision leads to small provision. A kingdom system will empower you to break through the ceiling of smallness and escape the system where we are just paying bills. There is a system behind being stuck in a cycle where we only have enough to meet our own immediate needs. This system puts us in a cycle that leaves no room for financial growth or increase. When our thoughts are influenced by the wrong system we will not have the liberty to create massive impact or influence in the influential spheres of society. It's time to break free from the system that's behind small vision and small provision.

Assessment:

a. What issues or challenges in your life are demanding most of your attention? How much time do you spend thinking and praying about these issues and or challenges? The will and intent of God must become a priority in your life. When we focus on our own personal needs as a priority, we violate the law of first things first. Monitor your thoughts over the course of the next few weeks in order to determine if the will and intent of God is really a priority. If it is not, you will have to put more pressure on your thought life in order to shift your focus. One way to do this is to keep a journal of kingdom communications. Record everything Holy Spirit says and reveals to you. Let this become the book you meditate on day and night (Joshua 1:8). You can never just stop thinking about something. You have to intentionally replace your thoughts with the thoughts of God (Philippians 4:8). Make a list of thoughts you need to replace. Now destroy that list and make a list of thoughts from the mind of God and meditate on those thoughts. The list of thoughts from the mind of God should not just be scriptures you've pulled from the bible apart from the leadership of Holy Spirit. These thoughts should be things Holy Spirit has said and revealed to you. Again, the goal is to remain submitted to the leadership of Holy Spirit.

_____
_____
_____
_____
_____
_____
_____
_____
_____
_____
_____

b. Kingdom manifestation requires appointed people and appointed things which move and serve according to their appointed role in the will of God. When Jesus turns the water into wine, everyone involved plays an appointed role. No one is asked to do anything they are not appointed to do. Even the 6 water pot system was appointed to be used. Ask Holy Spirit to reveal the Father's economic plan for the next 5 years of your life. The goal is to discover how provision is appointed to flow into your life. What systems are appointed to be used (stock market investments; real estate investments; small business etc.)

_____
_____
_____
_____
_____
_____

c. Develop a global vision for whatever you are appointed to do but build locally first. Write out your vision (1) for local impact, (2) to impact generations and (3) for global impact.

LESSON 7 - MANTLES AND MOTIVES

2 Corinthians 12:9-10 (NKJV)

[9] And He said to me, "My grace is sufficient for you, for My strength is made perfect in weakness." Therefore most gladly I will rather boast in my infirmities, that the power of Christ may rest upon me. [10] Therefore I take pleasure in infirmities, in reproaches, in needs, in persecutions, in distresses, for Christ's sake. For when I am weak, then I am strong.

1) Mantles can be inherited from biological family as well as passed on by apostolic or prophetic fathers (2 Timothy 1:3-5). Mantles are passed after the death or the elevation of someone who previously carried that mantle. Possessing a mantle also means that something is integrated in your life and flows naturally through your life. I received a mantle of endurance from my biological father. This mantle was first seen in the life of my grandfather Oscar, who as a farmer demonstrated extraordinary determination to accomplish his goals. That same extraordinary determination was seen in the life of my father, Warren who worked through severe pain in order to continue living a productive life. My father served and was a blessing to many with his handyman skills in spite of the adversity of the pain which he endured. I often hear the stories of how my dad would show up for repair jobs and his pain would be obvious. Sometimes he would sit in his truck and give instructions to a helper or he would just work through the pain in order to complete the job. This mantle of endurance was proven to be authentic by means of the level of productivity he was able to maintain while facing physical challenges.

2) The purpose of a mantle is to empower productivity beyond your own strength or ability. I've been the most productive through the years when I endured the greatest adversity. There were seasons in my life where the level of adversity I encountered was so intense that I questioned doing what I knew I had been sent to do. Holy Spirit would never release me to miss one assignment. He would always encourage me to lift my head and go do what I was sent to do. Amazingly, each time this happened I witnessed the impact that was made on someone's life. I had to learn to rely on the strength of God through the mantles given to me. Your gifts and grace are not impacted by any level of adversity. The prophetic mantle and the mantle of endurance will always work for me at any time or in any situation wherein I am appointed to serve. Adversity served to prove that my gifts and grace are authentic.

3) When it comes to proving the authenticity of a mantle, there must be some challenge that you face in life. The mantle is proven when you are able to maintain a high level of productivity or produce kingdom results in spite of what state you are in or what challenges you face. My prophetic mantle has been proven and regardless of what state you find me in, this mantle empowers me to be prophetically productive.

2 Kings 2:9-15 (NKJV)

⁹ And so it was, when they had crossed over, that Elijah said to Elisha, "Ask! What may I do for you, before I am taken away from you?"

Elisha said, "Please let a double portion of your spirit be upon me."

¹⁰ So he said, "You have asked a hard thing. Nevertheless, if you see me when I am taken from you, it shall be so for you; but if not, it shall not be so." ¹¹ Then it happened, as they continued on and talked, that suddenly a chariot of fire appeared with horses of fire, and separated the two of them; and Elijah went up by a whirlwind into heaven.

¹² And Elisha saw it, and he cried out, "My father, my father, the chariot of Israel and its horsemen!" So he saw him no more. And he took hold of his own clothes and tore them into two pieces. ¹³ He also took up the mantle of Elijah that had fallen from him, and went back and stood by the bank of the Jordan. ¹⁴ Then he took the mantle of Elijah that had fallen from him, and struck the water, and said, "Where is the LORD God of Elijah?" And when he also had struck the water, it was divided this way and that; and Elisha crossed over.

¹⁵ Now when the sons of the prophets who were from[a] Jericho saw him, they said, "The spirit of Elijah rests on Elisha." And they came to meet him, and bowed to the ground before him.

4) Crossing the Jordan represents a challenge Elisha would have to overcome in order to be effective in what he had been sent to do. The anointing and grace on our lives is only as effective as its ability to resolve problems in our own lives. Mantles should be proven in our own lives first. You can never release or impart a mantle that has not been proven in your own life first. Elijah had the answer to crossing the Jordan. If Elisha has this same mantle, he should be able to cross the Jordan too. Elisha proves the mantle is authentic by testing it on the Jordan. The sons of the prophets witnessed this kingdom result and knew Elisha had the mantle of Elijah.

2 Corinthians 12:7-10 (NKJV)

⁷ And lest I should be exalted above measure by the abundance of the revelations, a thorn in the flesh was given to me, a messenger of Satan to buffet me, lest I be exalted above measure. ⁸ Concerning this thing I pleaded with the Lord three times that it might depart from me. ⁹ And He said to me, "My grace is sufficient for you, for My strength is made perfect in weakness." Therefore most gladly I will rather boast in my infirmities, that the power of Christ may rest upon me. ¹⁰ Therefore I take pleasure in infirmities, in reproaches, in needs, in persecutions, in distresses, for Christ's sake. For when I am weak, then I am strong.

5) Having to endure seasons of adversity has taught me how to leverage adversity. I've learned that adversity is not something to pray away but something to use as leverage. The presence of adversity indicates there is something bigger that God has intended and for that reason adversity shows up. Most saints believe any form of opposition is from the enemy and there is a tendency to fight anything that opposes what we are trying to do or the direction we are trying to move in. These saints never consider that God has employed the enemy (Proverbs 16:4). When the children of Israel left Egypt and were confronted by the Red Sea while being pursued by Pharaoh and his armies, God gave two separate instructions. (1) stand still and (2) move forward. The instruction "stand still," pertained to the enemy and meant do not turn and engage this enemy. The instruction to "move forward" pertained to the will of God and meant keep moving forward in the direction of the will of God. Essentially what was happening is Pharaoh and his army had been employed by God to serve as a buffer for the will of God. In other words, had the children of Israel found themselves facing the enemy they would have known they were headed in the wrong direction. Pharaoh and his army, being employed by God, were summoned to pursue the children of Israel. Had the children of Israel turned to engage this enemy, they would have been engaged in a battle they would not have won. Adversity can be used as leverage to indicate alignment with the will and intent of God. Many times when adversity shows up we simply need to look deeper into the intent of God.

6) The process that leads to the formation of God's vision in our hearts aligns our gifts with the intent of God. The intent of God comes down to what God wants versus what we want and or need. It is the intent of God to meet all of our needs but not at the expense of His purpose and intent being unfulfilled in the earth. Many serve their own agenda using their gifts by doing whatever they want to do, like to do or are asked to do. The need for provision dictates many of the decisions we make pertaining to how we appropriate time, energy, focus gifts and grace. This approach violates a primal kingdom law given to us in Matthew 6:25-34. Gifts are for kingdom service. Anointing is for kingdom results.

7) In the process of aligning our gifts with the intent of God our motives are proven. Elisha had to endure the process of walking away from his livelihood in order to follow Elijah. Nothing they were involved in has anything to do with a personal agenda, yet Elisha doesn't quit. The intent of everything Elisha does with Elijah is to serve someone else. Elisha is learning how to serve the intent of God first. This is a kingdom model that we must follow if we are going to build effectively in the kingdom of God. This model will prove motives as we go through the process of reconciling our dreams with God's vision.

8) Elijah and Elisha were productive in the will of God and in serving the intent of God as they visited prophetic schools in Gilgal, Bethel, Jericho and at the Jordan. These schools were established by Samuel and Elijah's model was to visit each of these schools on a circuit to fulfill the intent of God. This proved to be a productive model for Elijah and Elisha caught this model. Elisha understood how to be productive in the will of God and how to serve the intent of God as a priority in his life. The Kingdom of God rewards our productivity in the will of God as we serve the intent of God.

John 7:6-10 (NKJV)

⁶ Then Jesus said to them, "My time has not yet come, but your time is always ready. ⁷ The world cannot hate you, but it hates Me because I testify of it that its works are evil. ⁸ You go up to this feast. I am not yet going up to this feast, for My time has not yet fully come." ⁹ When He had said these things to them, He remained in Galilee. ¹⁰ But when His brothers had gone up, then He also went up to the feast, not openly, but as it were in secret.

9) Gifts, grace and or anointing alone do not justify any action or response. Jesus was gifted, graced and anointed to do great and mighty works at this feast but He never did anything just because He was graced to do it. Jesus only did what He saw the Father doing. He always remained loyal to the purpose and intent of God the Father. Gifts, grace and anointing must always be appropriated according to the will, purpose, intent and plan of God. There will always be a lot of things you could do because you are gifted and graced but the question will always be, "(1) is this my assignment (2) is this how the Father has purposed me to appropriate His grace on my life (3) what/where is the Father's intent in this? The Kingdom of God is a higher call to a greater level of service. That service first and foremost is to the Father's purpose and intent for your life. We must always remain loyal to the purpose and intent of God.

Assessment:

a. What are some of the greatest challenges you've faced in life? What was the key to overcoming those challenges?

_____
_____
_____
_____
_____
_____
_____
_____
_____

b. What gifts or grace has been proven to be authentic in your life by means of the challenges you've faced and overcome?

_____
_____
_____
_____
_____
_____
_____
_____
_____

c. What lessons has adversity taught you? Are there some things you've been trying to pray away but yet they remain? What are they? The adversity that you are experiencing now could indicate there is a deeper dimension to your gifts and grace that you've not yet discovered. Meditate on 2 Corinthians 12:7-13. Ask Holy Spirit to reveal any dimensions of grace that lie dormant in your life.

LESSON 8 - KINGDOM REWARDS

1 Corinthians 9:1-18 (NKJV)

9 Am I not an apostle? Am I not free? Have I not seen Jesus Christ our Lord? Are you not my work in the Lord? ² If I am not an apostle to others, yet doubtless I am to you. For you are the seal of my apostleship in the Lord.

³ My defense to those who examine me is this: ⁴ Do we have no right to eat and drink? ⁵ Do we have no right to take along a believing wife, as do also the other apostles, the brothers of the Lord, and Cephas? ⁶ Or is it only Barnabas and I who have no right to refrain from working? ⁷ Who ever goes to war at his own expense? Who plants a vineyard and does not eat of its fruit? Or who tends a flock and does not drink of the milk of the flock?

⁸ Do I say these things as a mere man? Or does not the law say the same also? ⁹ For it is written in the law of Moses, "You shall not muzzle an ox while it treads out the grain." Is it oxen God is concerned about? ¹⁰ Or does He say it altogether for our sakes? For our sakes, no doubt, this is written, that he who plows should plow in hope, and he who threshes in hope should be partaker of his hope. ¹¹ If we have sown spiritual things for you, is it a great thing if we reap your material things? ¹² If others are partakers of this right over you, are we not even more? Nevertheless we have not used this right, but endure all things lest we hinder the gospel of Christ. ¹³ Do you not know that those who minister the holy things eat of the things of the temple, and those who serve at the altar partake of the offerings of the altar? ¹⁴ Even so the Lord has commanded that those who preach the gospel should live from the gospel.

¹⁵ But I have used none of these things, nor have I written these things that it should be done so to me; for it would be better for me to die than that anyone should make my boasting void. ¹⁶ For if I preach the gospel, I have nothing to boast of, for necessity is laid upon me; yes, woe is me if I do not preach the gospel! ¹⁷ For if I do this willingly, I have a reward; but if against my will, I have been entrusted with a stewardship. ¹⁸ What is my reward

then? That when I preach the gospel, I may present the gospel of Christ without charge, that I may not abuse my authority in the gospel.

1) Apostle Paul shows us a ministry model that's based on a kingdom reward system. The Kingdom of God rewards us for being productive in the will of God as we serve the intent of God. Anything that has no connection to the intent of God for your life is work. A work based system is not a kingdom system. Compensation for a work based system is based on your physical presence and performance. The purpose of work therefore is to discover gifts, grace and assignment. Once we discover our gifts, grace and assignment through the work we've chosen, we need to transition into a field, genre or space where we can serve in order to fulfill our assignment and the intent of God.

Deuteronomy 11:10-14 (NKJV)

[10] For the land which you go to possess is not like the land of Egypt from which you have come, where you sowed your seed and watered it by foot, as a vegetable garden; [11] but the land which you cross over to possess is a land of hills and valleys, which drinks water from the rain of heaven, [12] a land for which the LORD your God cares; the eyes of the LORD your God are always on it, from the beginning of the year to the very end of the year.

[13] 'And it shall be that if you earnestly obey My commandments which I command you today, to love the LORD your God and serve Him with all your heart and with all your soul, [14] then I will give you the rain for your land in its season, the early rain and the latter rain, that you may gather in your grain, your new wine, and your oil.

2) Kingdom service maximizes the investment of the Father's grace in our lives. Anything we do that has no connection to the intent of God or that does not place demands on our gifts and or grace is classified as work. Many people work all of their lives and never discover what they were really appointed to do. Work becomes unfruitful whenever that work does not lead to some level of service in the kingdom of God. The kingdom of God rewards based on our level of productivity in the will of God. Rewards can come in a number of different ways and we are not physically involved in everything we receive. Productivity in the will of God in order to fulfill the intent of God is what primarily drives kingdom rewards. Serving the intent of God has benefits.

3) Paul's rewards were so great he didn't need to receive honorariums. He was able to support those who traveled with him on just the kingdom rewards he received. Paul also served the population at large through his tent making business so kingdom rewards could flow into his life through his business. In Paul's ministry model, honorariums were increase. Increase is over the top of what you need to maintain your lifestyle.
4) There needs to be a pathway for increase and kingdom reward to flow consistently into our lives through something outside of our appointed service. Everything the kingdom of God manifests, wants to flow consistently in and through our lives. There needs to be a connection to something outside of our assignment to serve. If not, we will expect our service to produce a level of increase that service is not appointed to produce. This is when we start expecting and making demands to be compensated for every level of service we provide. We take on a "get paid" mentality when it comes to service and this does not represent a kingdom model.
5) When Jesus turned the water into wine, He responded to the request of His mother by saying, "what does this have to do with Me," because this went beyond service. We have to understand how to move beyond service in order to produce the provision needed in order to do the things we should be able to do. We should be able to get married, start families and live productive family lives. In verse 5 of 1 Corinthians 9, Paul declares that we have a right to support our families. We simply need to follow a kingdom model in order to do this the right way.
6) In John 2:1-11, everyone plays an appointed role. The disciples were there to learn and they are not asked to handle the water or the wine. The servants are there to serve and they are the only ones asked to handle the provision of water and wine. Jesus is there to direct the flow of provision. He displaces the master of the feast who previously filled that role in order to shift the system of the water pots so that the kingdom of God could flow through that system. Jesus never asked anyone to do anything they were not appointed to do. When we do not follow a kingdom model we look to people to do what they are not appointed to do and leaders start placing demands on servants to serve in a capacity they are not appointed to serve.

2 Kings 4:1-7 (NKJV)

4 A certain woman of the wives of the sons of the prophets cried out to Elisha, saying, "Your servant my husband is dead, and you know that your servant feared the LORD. And the creditor is coming to take my two sons to be his slaves." ² So Elisha said to her, "What shall I do for you? Tell me, what do you have in the house?" And she said, "Your maidservant has nothing in the house but a jar of oil." ³ Then he said, "Go, borrow vessels

from everywhere, from all your neighbors—empty vessels; do not gather just a few. **4** And when you have come in, you shall shut the door behind you and your sons; then pour it into all those vessels, and set aside the full ones." **5** So she went from him and shut the door behind her and her sons, who brought the vessels to her; and she poured it out. **6** Now it came to pass, when the vessels were full, that she said to her son, "Bring me another vessel." And he said to her, "There is not another vessel." So the oil ceased. **7** Then she came and told the man of God. And he said, "Go, sell the oil and pay your debt; and you and your sons live on the rest."

7) The widow whose husband is now deceased tapped into supernatural increase. But before she sold anything, her oil supernaturally multiplied. The multiplication of the oil was a kingdom reward that was due as result of her husband's service. The man who was given the 5 talents was also rewarded for being productive (Matthew 25:28, 29). It is a violation in the kingdom not to be rewarded for being productive in the appointed things of God (Hebrews 6:10). In the Kingdom of God, increase follows kingdom rewards. If you are only receiving rewards through honorariums, there needs to be system set up for kingdom increase to flow into your life.

Assessment:

a. In order to be effective in the kingdom of God, you cannot be uncertain about (1) what's most important to God, (2) what God requires of you and (3) what is the single most important thing you do in the will of God in a given season (1 Corinthians 9:26). With each season of life you must resolve based on kingdom communications, what is the single most important thing you do in the will of God. This decision will determine how you appropriate the primary currencies of time, energy and focus. Whenever you are involved with the will of God you must bring your best energy and focus. How are you investing your time, energy and focus right now? What adjustments are required in order to align with the will and intent of God for this season of your life? Are you tired or do you struggle to focus when doing what is the single most important thing in the will of God? If so, this is a clear indicator that some adjustments are required in how you appropriate time, energy and focus.

_____

_____

_____

_____

_____

b. It is possible to get so caught up in serving those you are appointed to serve that you miss an appointment to build what you appointed to build that will serve to be a means of provision for your family over the course of the next 5-10 years. Once your service level grace is set up you should begin to ask Holy Spirit about the Father's plan for your life beyond service. This is called systems level grace. Service level grace flows through and to people. Systems level grace flows through systems. Revisit the Father's economic plan for your life. Ask Holy Spirit for greater clarity and understanding regarding how provision is appointed to flow into and through your life.

LESSON 9 - GIVING AND RECEIVING

Luke 12:35-48 (NKJV)

³⁵ "Let your waist be girded and your lamps burning; ³⁶ and you yourselves be like men who wait for their master, when he will return from the wedding, that when he comes and knocks they may open to him immediately. ³⁷ Blessed are those servants whom the master, when he comes, will find watching. Assuredly, I say to you that he will gird himself and have them sit down to eat, and will come and serve them. ³⁸ And if he should come in the second watch, or come in the third watch, and find them so, blessed are those servants. ³⁹ But know this, that if the master of the house had known what hour the thief would come, he would [a]have watched and not allowed his house to be broken into. ⁴⁰ Therefore you also be ready, for the Son of Man is coming at an hour you do not expect." ⁴¹ Then Peter said to Him, "Lord, do You speak this parable only to us, or to all people?"

⁴² And the Lord said, "Who then is that faithful and wise steward, whom his master will make ruler over his household, to give them their portion of food [b]in due season? ⁴³ Blessed is that servant whom his master will find so doing when he comes. ⁴⁴ Truly, I say to you that he will make him ruler over all that he has. ⁴⁵ But if that servant says in his heart, 'My master is delaying his coming,' and begins to beat the male and female servants, and to eat and drink and be drunk, ⁴⁶ the master of that servant will come on a day when he is not looking for him, and at an hour when he is not aware, and will cut him in two and appoint him his portion with the unbelievers. ⁴⁷ And that servant who knew his master's will, and did not prepare himself or do according to his will, shall be beaten with many stripes. ⁴⁸ But he who did not know, yet committed things deserving of stripes, shall be beaten with few. For everyone to whom much is given, from him much will be required; and to whom much has been committed, of him they will ask the more.

1) Being considered a wise and faith steward involves having a vision to serve the population at large by means of the gifts and grace the Father has invested in us. This requires stewardship of our assignment as well as the primary currencies of time, energy and focus. Once we are consistently productive in our assignment, our lives will begin to reap the benefits of purpose and intent being fulfilled through us.

Holy Spirit will direct the flow of provision into our lives once we serve the intent of God as the priority for our lives. This redirection of provision releases servants (diakonos) or those who are appointed to serve into our lives to serve. "Diakonos" is the Greek word used for deacon. These servants are appointed to serve those who serve the intent of God in the earth realm. This account shows that these positions and offices to include 5-fold ministry gifts were given as a model. It was never the Father's intent that these offices, functions and roles be diminished to just a role in what we call church.

Philippians 4:10-20 (NKJV)

[10] But I rejoiced in the Lord greatly that now at last your care for me has flourished again; though you surely did care, but you lacked opportunity. [11] Not that I speak in regard to need, for I have learned in whatever state I am, to be content: [12] I know how to be abased, and I know how to abound. Everywhere and in all things I have learned both to be full and to be hungry, both to abound and to suffer need. [13] I can do all things through Christ who strengthens me.

[14] Nevertheless you have done well that you shared in my distress. [15] Now you Philippians know also that in the beginning of the gospel, when I departed from Macedonia, no church shared with me concerning giving and receiving but you only. [16] For even in Thessalonica you sent aid once and again for my necessities. [17] Not that I seek the gift, but I seek the fruit that abounds to your account. [18] Indeed I have all and abound. I am full, having received from Epaphroditus the things sent from you, a sweet-smelling aroma, an acceptable sacrifice, well pleasing to God. [19] And my God shall supply all your need according to His riches in glory by Christ Jesus. [20] Now to our God and Father be glory forever and ever. Amen.

2) "Diakonos" or deacons who are appointed to serve, show up once we are in a receive position. The receive position is a position of agreement and alignment with the intent of God. Your receive position is a position from which you serve what you carry to those you are appointed to serve. From this position we participate in giving as well as receiving.

James 4:2 (NKJV)

[2] You lust and do not have. You murder and covet and cannot obtain. You fight and war. Yet you do not have because you do not ask.

3) The law of asking is activated when we ask specifically and precisely according to the intent of God. We must see into the intent of the Father's heart in order to activate this law. Over the course of several years Holy Spirit revealed the Father's intent for me to invest. I studied stock investments, talked about stock investments, attended seminars and even shared about the Father's intent for my life to become an investor. But I never executed the will of God to move into a receive position to become an investor. As a result I never received any detailed instructions concerning this. There were some details I overlooked and failed to execute. One detail was to invest in the lives of those I am appointed to serve first. This is being done through the publication of this course. Even though I am set up to begin investing, none of my investments would work until I made this investment first. With the completion of this course, I will be in the receive position and detailed instructions will flow through Holy Spirit leading me into becoming a successful investor.

4) **_"We have not because we ask not"_** – we've interpreted this part of the scripture from a fallen paradigm and as a result we've come up with the wrong conclusion which means we are not able to execute the will of God when it comes to the law of asking. God is not dealing with asking for things right here. This part of the scripture deals with consistently asking for direction and guidance from Holy Spirit in order to get into position to receive and have things added to our lives. We must be consistent in being led by Holy Spirit (Romans 8:14) in order to be led into a receive position (Revelation 22:17). From the receive position we ask and the things we ask are added to our lives.

5) **_"We ask and do not receive because we ask amiss"_** – there are two different Greek words that are translated to the English word "ask." "Aiteo" is the petition of one who is in a lesser position than the one to whom the petition is made. "Erotao" suggests that the petitioner is on a level of equality or familiarity with the person he is making the request of. Jesus never used "aiteo" in making request to the Father. He always used "erotao" which indicates He always asked from a place of agreement and alignment with the intent of the Father's heart. In other words, He was always in the receive position whenever He asked. We are led into the receive position by means of being led by Holy Spirit. The Kingdom of God is the uninterrupted flow of the will of God in and through our life. When we are not in alignment with the intent of God, that flow is restricted and perhaps obstructed. The receive position is a position of agreement and alignment with the intent of the Father's heart. The Kingdom will flow freely into our lives from this position.

6) Many saints are confused when it comes to timing. Seedtime is a principle that governs what happens based on my involvement and participation (Genesis 8:22). This principle is seed plus time. I am responsible for seed which is my contribution to the will of God. I am also accountable for time. In other words, I am responsible for how I respond or my contribution and or obligation to the will of God. I am also

accountable for the timing in which I respond in order to fulfill my obligation to the will of God. Our response to the will of God dictates the timing of what happens here in the earth realm. If we are slow resolving a response to the will of God, provision will be slow or show up late based on the principle of seedtime and harvest. Seed + time = harvest.

7) A set time is created once we execute the will of God to move into a receive position. This is where we create opportunities for those who are appointed to serve us to do what they are appointed to do for us. Once the set time is created, appointed people, appointed places and appointed things line up and we begin to see sudden manifestations of provision in our life. We are accountable for time. We are accountable for the time that it takes us to execute the will of God in order to move into a receive position. Never wait on a set time. A set time is created to meet God's appointment by means of executing the will of God in the now moment of your life.

8) Much of what begins to manifest and show up in your life at set the time has been redirected to you by Holy Spirit. Holy Spirit will shift and release people to do something different with their seed, tithes and offerings. You are being rewarded for being a faithful and a wise steward. "Diakonos" or deacons can't do anything until they are given an instruction or command. True servants only move by instruction or command because they have to be released to do what they are appointed to do. There are different levels of servants who serve from different dimensions. "Diakonos" is a person who is appointed to serve in the earth realm.

Psalm 103:19-22 (NKJV)

[19] The LORD has established His throne in heaven, And His kingdom rules over all. [20] Bless the LORD, you His angels, Who excel in strength, who do His word, Heeding the voice of His word. [21] Bless the LORD, all you His hosts, You ministers of His, who do His pleasure. [22] Bless the LORD, all His works, In all places of His dominion. Bless the LORD, O my soul!

9) Another level of servants in the kingdom of God are angelic hosts. Hosts is the Hebrew word "tabaah," which means a mass of persons or things organized for war; an army. "Tabaah" is a combination of appointed time + army + battle. This scripture text speaks to the Government of God appointed to serve the intent of God. Agents of the Government of God are also referred to as "ministers" which means to attend, contribute or wait upon. This level of supernatural support is available to those who serve the intent of God. Angelic hosts do not serve us. They are agents of the Government of God and wait upon or serve the intent of God. These agents therefore will never be manipulated by men.

1 Samuel 17:45 (NKJV)

⁴⁵ Then David said to the Philistine, "You come to me with a sword, with a spear, and with a javelin. But I come to you in the name of the LORD of hosts, the God of the armies of Israel, whom you have defied. ⁴⁶ This day the LORD will deliver you into my hand, and I will strike you and take your head from you. And this day I will give the carcasses of the camp of the Philistines to the birds of the air and the wild beasts of the earth, that all the earth may know that there is a God in Israel.

> 10) When we challenge the systems that stand in the way of the intent of God, supernatural support shows up. David confronted Goliath in the name of the Lord of Hosts. These hosts are agents of the Government of God. David declares that the Government of God or the Hosts will bring Goliath down. David prevails with a sling shot and a stone. The sling shot and stone represent David's kingdom system. The Government of God worked through this kingdom system to bring Goliath down. David challenged the systems of the world through his kingdom system which caused supernatural support to show up. Supernatural support showed up once David challenged the system that defied the Government of God.

Assessment:

a. What is a real need in your life right now? Has Holy Spirit talked to you specifically about this need? The widow in 1 Kings 17 had to see pass her own immediate need in order to see into the intent of God. Are you able to see past this need? If not, you most likely are not seeing into the intent of God either. The answer to your need is how you respond to the intent of God. Detailed instructions are given once you are in a receive position to fulfill the intent of God. Provision for your need will be attached to that. So what do you see?

_____
_____
_____
_____
_____
_____

b. What do you feel God really wants from you at this point? What must you do in order to satisfy the requirements of what God wants? Ask Holy Spirit for clarity and understanding.

LESSON 10 - SENT DIMENSION

Psalm 103:19-22 (NKJV)

¹⁹ The LORD has established His throne in heaven, And His kingdom rules over all. ²⁰ Bless the LORD, you His angels, Who excel in strength, who do His word, Heeding the voice of His word. ²¹ Bless the LORD, all you His hosts, You ministers of His, who do His pleasure. ²² Bless the LORD, all His works, In all places of His dominion.
Bless the LORD, O my soul!

1) The word "sent" is the Greek word "apostollo." Sent therefore is apostolic and governmental. We are sent once Holy Spirit gives His consent. Any reference to where Jesus went or what He did always uses the term sent and not called. In a called dimension, what we are asked to do by others has the greatest influence on what we believe we should be doing to fulfill the will of God. Many are called so many are doing what they assume God wants them to do because this is what people keep asking them to do (Matthew 22:14). Few are chosen. The chosen have gone through a process that eliminates everything God has not sent them to do. The sent dimension is composed of a specific territory or space as well as a specific assignment to an appointed people in that territory or space. The wilderness represents John the Baptist assigned space. His assignment was to introduce the message of the Kingdom of God in this space. John attracted those who were appointed to receive his revelation of the Kingdom of God in this appointed space. John is in an appointed space, preaching an authentic message to fulfill a specific assignment with the appointed people who came out to meet him in that space. John was in his sent dimension.

2) Being sent comes with consent from Holy Spirit. Consent from Holy Spirit is authorization from the CEO of all the affairs of the Kingdom of God in the earth realm. This authorization is required in order for the Kingdom of Heaven or Government of God to get involved. The church is impotent whenever we move without consent from Holy Spirit. Consent comes with instructions from Holy Spirit. Revelation reveals or opens something up but instruction gives the release to do something. Unless instructions are included, revelation doesn't always authorize me to act or move. We have no authority over any worldly systems or any natural laws without Holy Spirit's consent. Without His consent the outcome will be limited to what I can produce in my own strength.

1 Samuel 17:28 (NKJV)

²⁸ Now Eliab his oldest brother heard when he spoke to the men; and Eliab's anger was aroused against David, and he said, "Why did you come down here? And with whom have you left those few sheep in the wilderness? I know your pride and the insolence of your heart, for you have come down to see the battle."

3) In order to operate in a sent dimension you have to be able to weigh the difference between what you are asked to do and what you are sent to do. David was asked to bring supplies to his brothers but he was sent to slay Goliath. Once he arrived on the battlefield, what he was sent to do took precedence over what he had been asked to do. David's brother Eliab was offended and basically told him "no one asked you to get involved in this." In other words, stay in your lane. Your sent dimension is not a lane but a territory or space in which you've been sent to challenge systems, solve problems and have dominion. We are active in our sent dimension without an invite from man. We are processed by the intent of God which prepares us to be released into our sent dimension. As a result of the process that eliminates everything we may have thought we were supposed to do and also a lot of things people are asking us to do, we see and recognize the intent of God as life plays out before us. We are clear on what we've been sent to do and we understand the cause and the outcome we are sent to produce.
4) The sent dimension is a place of His dominion or what I call a kingdom government zone. The systems that challenge us where we are sent, defy the Government of God. This includes religious systems that want to occupy space assigned to you. You will experience and see the Government of God show up where you are sent because where you are sent is a Kingdom Government zone. The Government of God will manifest to move people and things out of your way and to supernaturally manifest support as you challenge these systems that stand in the way of the intent of God and what you've been sent to do.

Genesis 18:16-19 (NKJV)

¹⁶ Then the men rose from there and looked toward Sodom, and Abraham went with them to send them on the way. ¹⁷ And the LORD said, "Shall I hide from Abraham what I am doing, ¹⁸ since Abraham shall surely become a great and mighty nation, and all the nations of the earth shall be blessed in him? ¹⁹ For I have known him, in order that he may command his children and his household after him, that they keep the way of the LORD, to do

righteousness and justice, that the LORD may bring to Abraham what He has spoken to him."

5) Once we are processed by the intent of God we are given a seat at the table with the Government of God as a high ranking ambassador of the Kingdom of God where we are made privy to kingdom initiatives in our assigned regions or space. Abraham was this type of high ranking ambassador in the Government of God. Abraham was made privy to what God wanted to do in that region. Abraham had a seat at the table of the Government of God. High ranking ambassadors serve as gatekeepers in their assigned region. They are made privy to the spiritual movement in that region. Their decrees, declarations and prayers are used by the Hosts to shut or open doors in that region. Some of the meetings that get cancelled or conferences that get moved are not just a result of a leader changing their mind. Many times these meetings are interrupted by the Government of God because they are not in line with or will not serve the intent of God. High ranking ambassadors are not only made privy to this type of movement but they are also involved through their declarations and decrees in shutting down events that will not serve the intent of God.

6) Reference to high ranking ambassadors is not consistent with a title or office held in church. Again, leaders who are high ranking ambassadors have been processed by the intent of God. Their motives are in line with the intent of God and those things that are most important to God. Every Apostle, Bishop, Prophet, Evangelist, Pastor or Teacher will not have a seat at the table of the Government of God. Every 5-fold ministry leader is not made privy to high level movement in their assigned region.

Assessment:

a. What types of things are people consistently asking you to do and what has been the impact, the results or fruit of you being involved in those things over the course of time?

_____
_____
_____
_____
_____
_____

b. What is getting interrupted in your life? What does Holy Spirit lead you to do once He has interrupted you? How long does it take you to make the shift to what He is leading you to do? What unfruitful works do you need to eliminate from your life?

_____
_____
_____
_____
_____
_____
_____
_____
_____
_____

c. How much are you resisting Holy Spirit (Acts 7:51)? When we hit a ceiling in something we are appointed to do, this indicates a shift to another level or another dimension wants to take place. A shift to another level or dimension requires a shift in one or more of the three primary currencies of time, energy and focus. What are some things you are doing, not because Holy Spirit has given His consent or led you to do them, but you are doing these things just for the sake of doing something or perhaps you've seen someone else doing these things? Your why for anything you do must be in line with the intent of God. Let's identify your why.

_____
_____
_____
_____
_____
_____
_____
_____
_____

LESSON 11 - APOSTOLIC ORDER

1 Corinthians 12:28 (NKJV)

²⁸ And God has appointed these in the church: first apostles, second prophets, third teachers, after that miracles, then gifts of healings, helps, administrations, varieties of tong

1) This apostolic governmental model is given to be used as a pattern to set kingdom order in our lives, businesses, organizations and ministries. Isaiah 9:6 says the Government will be upon His shoulders. The head rests upon the shoulders so the head represents the Government. David cut off Goliath's head representing an overthrow of an opposing system governed by an opposing government. The apostolic dimension is a governmental dimension. Prophetic grace operates best within an apostolic dimension where an apostolic order has been set. Order is always set by what is appointed first. In an apostolic order, prophetic grace is a #2 grace appointed to serve in support of an apostolic assignment or what the apostle has been sent to build. It is not uncommon to see apostolic, prophetic and teaching grace in the life of one person. Grace is manifold or multi-dimensional therefore all of us have layers to our gifts and grace. Once we have a governmental order set in place we can expect governmental support which manifest in the form of a supernatural dimension of grace.

Ecclesiastes 3:14 (NKJV)

¹⁴ I know that whatever God does, It shall be forever.
Nothing can be added to it, And nothing taken from it.
God does *it*, that men should fear before Him.

2) God operates by appointment. Nothing can be added to or taken away from anything God has appointed. Adding or taking away from an appointment disrupts apostolic order resulting in the absence of a supernatural dimension of grace. Many leaders do not operate within an apostolic order and are just teaching and or preaching without an appointment or a cause. David's encounter with Goliath was an appointment that revealed a cause (1 Samuel 17:29). He wasn't asked to get involved but he was sent to challenge this system and this takes precedence over anything he had been asked to do. His gifts and grace align with this intent and his whole focus shifts to this one thing. Any other gift or grace he has in his life will primarily be invested in this cause and appointment. This is apostolic order that leads

to a supernatural dimension of Kingdom Governmental support.
3) Again, order is set by whatever is appointed first. An apostolic assignment or cause is appointed first in the church. 5-fold ministry offices, functions and roles were never intended by God to be diminished to just a function or role in what we call church. Kingdom manifestation will be limited when we have not set the correct order in our lives when it comes to appointment, gifts and grace.
4) The pattern we see with this model appoints an apostolic assignment or cause first. This means whatever we are sent to do must be first. The true gift of apostolic grace is grace to build. Apostle Paul called himself a wise master builder (1 Corinthians 3:10). At the apostolic level we must identify with a specific cause and whatever we build must be built to support that cause. Keep in mind, we are looking at this from the perspective of models and dimensions of grace and not offices. The cause relates to what we've been sent to do. Every kingdom leaders must identify with a specific cause. This cause represents your apostolic dimension. John the Baptist, the forerunner of the Kingdom, identified with a specific cause when he said," I am the voice of one crying in the wilderness. Prepare the way of the Lord," (John 1:19-23).
5) Next, prophetic grace is set in order. Prophetic grace is the systems engineering level of what we are appointed to build. This level of grace is appointed to support the apostolic appointment or what apostolic grace builds. Prophetic grace can be sent as well as set (Luke 4:25-27). There were many widows in Israel, but Elijah was sent to a widow in Zarephath in the region of Sidon. This speaks to the specific appointment of his gifts and grace. There were also many lepers in Israel but Naaman had to travel to the place where the Prophet Elisha was set. Many people fail to appropriate the grace that is appointed to serve them because they do not understand the kingdom law of appointment. When prophetic grace is sent the prophet has an apostolic appointment (Ezekiel 2:3-10). But when prophetic grace is set in an appointed place, that grace will support an apostolic assignment by means of developing and or shifting essential systems to support the intent of God.
6) The next layer in our model is teaching grace. This is a "diakonos" or service level grace and this layer may be either pastoral or teaching. This level of grace deals with how you will serve those you are appointed to serve. This is a practical dimension of grace that empowers your connection with your audience. This dimension of grace delivers a relevant message to support the cause.

7) A supernatural dimension of grace will flow through our gifts and grace once they are properly aligned with the intent of God. Engaging in something that does not utilize our gifts or grace and has no relevance to the intent of God or what He has sent us to do is classified as work in the kingdom of God. The purpose of work is to give us an opportunity to discover gifts, grace and the intent of God but it is not the intent of God that we work for our provision. It has always been the intent of God to add provision to our lives as a result of (1) serving His intent by means of our gifts and grace (2) leveraging gifts and grace to produce products and or systems that create pathways for provision to flow into our lives.

8) "Cause" is defined as something that gives rise to an action or movement. In an apostolic or kingdom order, cause takes precedence over message. The cause warrants certain things to be prioritized ahead of just a message. Once we understand the intent of God on an apostolic level, anything else we are gifted and graced to do must be done to support the cause and what we've been sent to do. The focus of kingdom leadership is not just a message but a cause. Once we set things in an apostolic order, the cause becomes more important than the message.

9) Great movements are not started by means of a message but by means of a cause. Martin Luther King Jr. led a movement because he had a cause. His message of love and equality was preached in support of the cause of civil rights. Civil rights was the movement or the cause. When you have a cause your strategy changes from just preaching and or teaching to building a platform to support a cause. This explains why teaching or pastoral grace, which deals with the message, is set in order after the apostolic assignment and the prophetic gifting and grace. With this kingdom model we don't build based on a message. Rather, we build based on an apostolic appointment or cause. A relevant kingdom message is used in support of the cause.

10) Leaders who do not identify with a specific cause get stuck in what I call conference mode. In conference mode the focus is on the message, not a cause. In conference

mode, our strategy consists of holding conferences and meetings that preach or teach a message but is lacking when it comes to a focus on social issues and community engagement. Our giveaways of food and or clothing will never start a movement that will result in sustainable change in our communities if not done in support of a specific cause. Like John the Baptist, we must identify with a specific cause (John 1:19-23) and that cause must be set first in the order of what we do.

1 Corinthians 4:20 (NKJV)

[20] For the kingdom of God *is* not in word but in power.

11) There is much debate over preaching the message of the kingdom versus preaching Jesus. There are those who emphasize that the kingdom of God was the only message Jesus preached or taught. Others argue that we should focus on preaching Jesus as the risen Savior of the world. Both arguments make valid points but once we understand apostolic order our perspective should change. The Kingdom of God is not in word only or is not just a message. The kingdom of God is an influence purposed to initiate a movement. The message of the kingdom of God must become a movement. Kingdom leaders who don't uphold any affiliation to any political or religious groups but who stand only for the Kingdom of God, are needed in this hour to initiate kingdom movements that are not only fueled by the message of the kingdom of God but are also focused on a specific cause.
12) Jesus was controversial because He was not affiliated with any of the political or religious groups of that day. Jesus was only influenced by the kingdom of God. This was the only influence, persuasion or affiliation He upheld. He was not Pentecostal, Charismatic, Baptist, COGIC, Lutheran, Catholic, Methodist, Full Gospel, Democratic, Republican, Independent etc. All of these as well as many others not mentioned represent some persuasion, influence or affiliation that does not fully embrace the kingdom of God. Jesus sent a strong message to the political and religious groups of that day that revealed where He stood. A distinction must be made that sends a strong message regarding who the real kingdom leaders are and where we stand. The message of the Kingdom of God will not have the impact it is purposed to have if we don't evolve with the message to become a movement. Your days of just talking about the kingdom and just teaching or preaching about the kingdom are over. You are appointed to evolve with the message of the kingdom to become a movement.
13) The power of God is absent from any form of ministry that never becomes a movement. The body of Christ is a moving, living organism. Any living organism or body that does not move over a period of time begins to slowly diminish and move

toward death. Pulpit ministry is not the best means of advancing the kingdom of God because this form of ministry lacks the power to initiate a movement. The church needs to focus on empowering kingdom citizens to get out into the spheres of society where decisions about the quality of life are being made and influence is happening. Influence is one of the most important and most powerful things that happens in the earth. Society is shaped by influence. Whoever has the greatest influence in the marketplaces of the world will have the greatest influence in the world.

14) Goliath immobilized the people of God because he exercised a level of influence over the leadership of the army of Israel. Saul was afraid of Goliath. Fear is a form of limited thinking. Here we begin to see the significance of influence when it comes to leadership. Leaders exercise the power of influence and leadership is a primary means through which influence takes place. Whenever we are learning, we are being influenced by whoever or whatever we've subjected our thoughts to. Learning shapes perspectives, behavior and responses which leads to the types of decisions that are made. Our lives are a result of the decisions we make on a daily basis. The influence of the kingdom changes the type of decisions we make as a result of leadership.

Ezekiel 37:1-14 (NKJV)

37 The hand of the LORD came upon me and brought me out in the Spirit of the LORD, and set me down in the midst of the valley; and it was full of bones. ² Then He caused me to pass by them all around, and behold, there were very many in the open valley; and indeed they were very dry. ³ And He said to me, "Son of man, can these bones live? So I answered, "O Lord GOD, You know."

⁴ Again He said to me, "Prophesy to these bones, and say to them, 'O dry bones, hear the word of the LORD! ⁵ Thus says the Lord GOD to these bones: "Surely I will cause breath to enter into you, and you shall live. ⁶ I will put sinews on you and bring flesh upon you, cover you with skin and put breath in you; and you shall live. Then you shall know that I am the LORD." ' "

⁷ So I prophesied as I was commanded; and as I prophesied, there was a noise, and suddenly a rattling; and the bones came together, bone to bone. ⁸ Indeed, as I looked, the sinews and the flesh came upon them, and the skin covered them over; but there was no breath in them.

[9] Also He said to me, "Prophesy to the breath, prophesy, son of man, and say to the breath, 'Thus says the Lord GOD: "Come from the four winds, O breath, and breathe on these slain, that they may live." ' " [10] So I prophesied as He commanded me, and breath came into them, and they lived, and stood upon their feet, an exceedingly great army.

15) The question that must be asked is how did the bones become dry. The word dry actually means "confused or disappointed." God is not the author of confusion (1 Corinthians 14:33). Any level of confusion indicates this is not God's system or God's sound. The term dry also speaks to a lack of an authentic visitation of the will of God. Whenever the will of God is not flowing through what we consistently subject our thoughts to, we can end up confused, disappointed and dry.

16) Ezekiel was told to prophesy to the dry bones or in other words release the sound of the will of God and say what you hear Holy Spirit saying to these dry bones. We have to check our sound or what we are saying about the issues we see and face in life. We have to monitor what we are contributing to the conversations we engage in about the issues we are sent to solve. Learn to ask questions in place of giving direct answers. God asked Ezekiel, can these bones live?" Ezekiel was mature enough not to answer based on what anyone could see. Ezekiel had walked with God long enough to understand the need to see what God sees. His response was based on a level of maturity. He essentially asks to see what God saw. Too many of us answer, respond and judge before we see what God sees. Questions are more effective than a direct statement when it comes to influence. If you really want to be influenced by the mind of God, ask Holy Spirit questions. The direct statements we are making to God should not outnumber the questions we are asking Holy Spirit.

17) Before Ezekiel was released to speak he needed to see what God saw. What he saw or was shown would enable him to tune his sound to the will of God. Essentially, this is how kingdom influence takes place. Whenever we are learning, we are being influenced by whoever or whatever we've subjected our thoughts to. But you cannot force knowledge or learning. Therefore a question is one of the most effective tools to use for influence.

18) Once Ezekiel released the sound of the will of God, the bones began to move. Now we have the start of a movement. The wrong sound will cause confusion and disappointment while a kingdom sound will bring an authentic visitation of the will of God to someone's life. The bones connected to the will of God once they were subjected to the right sound. Whenever we connect with the will and intent of God for our lives we will be led to connect with those who are under the influence of the same sound.

Assessment:

a. List at least 3 things you believe you are appointed to do. Now set them in order of significance and importance based on the overall will of God for your life. What will you commit to these things?

_____

_____

_____

_____

_____

_____

b. A kingdom sound will bring an authentic visitation of the will of God to someone's life. Anytime we believe we are in a dry place we should check the sound or influence we've subjected ourselves to. There are no dry seasons in the kingdom of God. A dry place indicates there has been no authentic visitation of the will of God in your life. Let's check the flow of the will of God and the flow of kingdom communications in and through our life. Kingdom communications is consistent. Each day when I sit down with Holy Spirit, within minutes I am in a flow of having my thoughts governed by Him and hearing what is on the Father's heart. Whenever this does not happen I know I've missed something in the will of God, my focus is not in the right place or I've not yet tapped into the stream of communications from the home country. Always take note when the flow of communications through Holy Spirit slows down, gets interrupted or ceases.

_____

_____

_____

_____

_____

_____

c. Let's do a sound check. We have to check our sound by monitoring what we are saying about the issues we see and face in life. We also have to monitor what we contribute to conversations about the issues we are sent to solve.

_____
_____
_____
_____
_____
_____
_____
_____

LESSON 12 - MULTI-DIMENSIONAL GRACE

Ephesians 4:7-16 (NKJV)

⁷ But to each one of us grace was given according to the measure of Christ's gift. ⁸ Therefore He says: "When He ascended on high, He led captivity captive, And gave gifts to men." ⁹ (Now this, "He ascended"—what does it mean but that He also [a]first descended into the lower parts of the earth? ¹⁰ He who descended is also the One who ascended far above all the heavens, that He might fill all things.) ¹¹ And He Himself gave some to be apostles, some prophets, some evangelists, and some pastors and teachers, ¹² for the equipping of the saints for the work of ministry, for the edifying of the body of Christ, ¹³ till we all come to the unity of the faith and of the knowledge of the Son of God, to a perfect man, to the measure of the stature of the fullness of Christ; ¹⁴ that we should no longer be children, tossed to and fro and carried about with every wind of doctrine, by the trickery of men, in the cunning craftiness of deceitful plotting, ¹⁵ but, speaking the truth in love, may grow up in all things into Him who is the head—Christ— ¹⁶ from whom the whole body, joined and knit together by what every joint supplies, according to the effective working by which every part does its share, causes growth of the body for the edifying of itself in love.

1) Grace is manifold or multi-dimensional (1 Peter 4:10). This means there are dimensions and layers to our gifts and grace. When it comes to the marketplace, we can no longer afford to operate with a juvenile understanding and fail to understand the dimensions of our gifts and grace. We need to know what apostolic, prophetic, evangelistic, pastoral and teaching grace look like in the marketplace. In the marketplace, dimensions of grace are more significant than a title or an office because the market places of this world will not acknowledge or recognize your title or office. The church is appointed to release kingdom citizens into the marketplace who are equipped with an understanding of their assignment and the dimensions of gifts they've been graced with for the purpose of fulfilling their assignment. The immature play church in the marketplace (Matthew 11:16, 17).

Dimensions of Grace

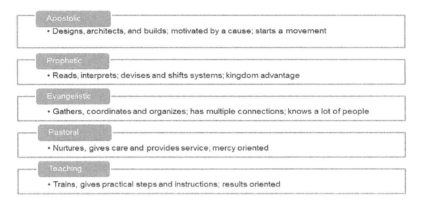

2) Keys to success in the kingdom: (1) understanding what is most important to God – Luke 5:1-11, (2) aligning your gifts and grace with the intent of God (3) stewarding your primary assignment by committing time, focus and energy to that which is most important to God. Essentially, this is how we present our bodies a living sacrifice (Romans 12:1). Our gifts and grace have a two-fold purpose. (1) serve the body or population at large. You are making life hard for someone when you withhold your gift. (2) Your gift was also given to serve or to take care of you. This is not something most of us have been taught and as a result we've believed that gifts are only appointed to serve in the church. Our gifts are a primary means God has given us to take care of us. Prominent leaders in the marketplace understand this and use their gifts as the means to live a life of abundance. We tend to think this is wrong and not the intent of God. Although there may be some problems with motives the concept in and of itself is consistent with the will of God. Over the last few years as I've studied the marketplace, I discovered a comedian who supports nine children and a team that travels with him, all on his gift to make people laugh. I also discovered a teacher who discovered his gift and was able to walk away from the classroom and now spends his time touring the country doing comedy shows for teachers. Laughter is medicine and makes the heart glad. These men are fulfilling purpose by means of their gift and are financially rewarded in the process. Their gifts are taking care of them and those with them.

3) Once we understand the dimensions of our gifts and grace we have to align those dimensions with the intent of God. Each dimension of our gifts and grace is appointed to serve those we are appointed to serve and or ourselves. There is a dimension of your gifts and grace appointed to cause increase to flow into your life.

1 Samuel 17:38-40 (NKJV)

⁴⁰ Then he took his staff in his hand; and he chose for himself five smooth stones from the brook, and put them in a shepherd's bag, in a pouch which he had, and his sling was in his hand. And he drew near to the Philistine.

4) David was gifted with skills to use the sling shot but we tend to overlook the small detail of his grace to select or choose the right stones. David's ability to find and choose smooth stones represents the prophetic layer of his gifts and grace. This is the layer where systems are developed to support the cause of what we've been sent to do. Systems level grace is key to a supernatural dimension of grace. Service level grace flows to and through servants, (diakonos) and or people. Systems level grace flows to and through systems.
5) Supernatural dimensions of grace are appointed to begin where service level dimensions of grace come up short or end. Prior to Jesus turning the water into wine, the bridegroom, master of the feast and servants all knew where the wine would come from because it manifested physically through the people who were appointed to provide the wine. Again, this was a service level, diakonos dimension of grace. They ran out of wine at a point where a supernatural dimension of grace was appointed to begin. Jesus navigated them through this shift in grace. An interruption to a flow of grace is an indication that a shift to a new dimension of grace is appointed to begin. Holy Spirit will navigate you through the shift to a new dimension of grace.
6) There is always a system involved when supernatural provision manifest. Jesus discerned that the man made 6 water pot system was appointed to be used to manifest supernatural provision. This is the same thing David did when he chose the 5 smooth stones and this is the role our gifts play when it comes to supernatural manifestation of grace. We find what has been appointed to be used by the Government of God in order to manifest a supernatural dimension of grace.

Ecclesiastes 10:5 (NKJV)

⁵ There is an evil I have seen under the sun, As an error proceeding from the ruler: Folly is set in great dignity while the rich sit in a lowly place.

7) The improper setting of gifts and grace is an error proceeding from the ruler or the one appointed to lead. This is a major problem in the traditional church model.

Heaven is a place where everything is specifically and precisely aligned with the intent of God. No one does anything in Heaven they were not appointed to do here in the earth. No one teaches or preaches who was never appointed to teach or preach. No one sings who was not appointed to sing. No one dances who was not appointed to dance. God operates His kingdom strictly by appointment and no one does anything they were not appointed to do. There is also nothing broken in heaven so the myth that someone will go to heaven to be a repairman is just that, a myth. To even imply that God has a need in His kingdom that requires Him to take a family member in order to fulfill is a serious indictment against and devaluation of God. This is the type of ignorance we must eliminate. Kingdom leaders should have zero tolerance for ignorance in the church. Every gift is set in order according to the original intent and purpose of God and the purpose of our kingdom model is to make earth look like heaven.

8) In order to be effective in kingdom building we must move past the traditional models that were handed down to us by our forefathers. We must embrace kingdom models and build ministries, businesses, organizations, families and marriages based on a kingdom model. Jesus spoke of a "rock" upon which He declared the church would be built (Matthew 16:16-18). The rock speaks to both stability and sustainability. Anything that is not built by means of a kingdom model will diminish and decline in its ability to have an impact in the changing world in which we live. The cover of this book has an image of what appears to a cave or a system of rocks. The intent was to illustrate the need to develop kingdom systems that model the kingdom of God. Traditional models will remain because many will fail to make the shift but the evidence of that which is built based on a kingdom model will be seen in the effectiveness, the impact and the influence that is sustained in spite of everything else changing. What is commonly referred to as the Joshua generation represents an upgrade to the current church model. The next generation of Kingdom leaders will be ushered in through this upgraded Kingdom model.

9) The apostolic appointment of the Prophet Ezekiel sent him to people God called "exiles," (Ezekiel 2:2-3 – 3:11). Exiles live outside of the Home Country. These are people who are held captive by leaders who missed the shift to a leadership style focused on a kingdom model. Apostles are revolutionaries who upset the order of former things. Apostles should expect to be met with some level of opposition when it comes to what they've been sent to build. Expect to encounter some level of opposition once you began to initiate a movement based on your apostolic cause. We must liberate the next generation of emerging kingdom leaders from a past move of God.

10) The rest of God is the best of God or His perfect will for our lives. Those who enter the rest of God cease from their own works (Hebrews 4:1-11). If we can ever deduce life to only what has been appointed by God with nothing added and nothing missing, we will enter the rest of God and live the best life now. The challenge is in ceasing from our own works. Essentially this means we have to go through a process where we get disconnected from the things we chose for ourselves but that were never things God appointed for us. This process brings us to an end of ourselves. The Kingdom of God begins where we end so this is a process wherein we die to self. Many people fight this process by means of holding on to former things. Former things block appointed things. The purpose of God will hide behind the things we have in our lives that are not appointed by Him. Once we abandon former things and shift to the appointed things, appointed people who are assigned to participate in the giving and receiving of what God is doing in our lives begin to show up.

Assessment:

a. What dimensions of grace are evident in your life? Describe what this grace looks like on your life in the marketplace.

_____
_____
_____
_____
_____
_____
_____
_____
_____
_____
_____
_____

b. You will not be able to fulfill purpose or the overall will of God in a single field, genre or sphere. Be courageous and explore opportunities outside of the field where you discovered your gifts and grace. The men who were productive, traded with their talents (Matthew 25:14-30). Trading takes you into the unknown where you will sometimes be required to learn new skills in order to repackage your gifts and grace or reinvent yourself. Most of us spend more than enough time in church. Let's explore the marketplace. This is where real influence takes place. Whoever has the greatest influence in the marketplace will have the greatest influence and impact in the world. Ask Holy Spirit to give you a vision to impact and influence the marketplace.

_____

_____

_____

_____

_____

_____

_____

_____

_____

_____

c. Emerging kingdom leaders explore opportunities to advance the kingdom. They effectively expand beyond the boundaries and limitations of their previous situation by means of accepting the challenge of expansion into a new field, genre or sphere. How much of a risk taker are you? At some point you will be required to jump into your purpose and your destiny. Many dibble and dabble in their purpose while holding onto former things for financial support. We cannot present our bodies as a living sacrifice to do the will of God if we can never position ourselves to offer our best time, energy and focus to the will of God. When we dibble and dabble with purpose what we bring to the table is only whatever time, energy and focus is left after we've given our best to the work we've chosen to do for our own provision. God didn't want what was left of Peter's time, energy and focus after Peter had been out fishing all day. The will of God created an opportunity for Peter to walk away (Luke 5:11). Now he will be able to give God his best in time, energy and focus. The purpose and intent of God wants to consume us to the point of dominating our life. Everything in life should revolve around the intent of God for our life. God abandons the first in order to establish the second (Hebrews 10:9). The first is what we've chosen and God uses that until we discover what He has appointed. At that point, it is time to jump. What's keeping you from jumping?

MASTER BUILDERS MASTERY COURSE

CONCLUSION

A defining moment happened in my life in 2011 when I found myself hospitalized as a result of a blood clot that moved into my lung. The blood clot compromised my ability to breath and even though the treatment to cause the clot to dissolve could be administered by myself at home, I was not allowed to leave the hospital until my breathing returned to a normal level. The Lord visited me in the hospital and asked me a question. He said to me, if you knew you only had so much time left, how would that impact the approach you take toward what you are doing? At first, I was somewhat disturbed by the question but after a day or two I realized I needed to give an answer to this question in order to get released from the hospital. At this point, it was not my compromised breathing that was keeping me there, but it was a need for greater clarity on the intent of God. I was being detained due to a lack of clarity.

Upon realizing what the Lord was requiring of me, I began to ponder the question He had asked as well as how things in my ministry life were moving at that time and I came to some conclusions. First of all, I resolved that I was not satisfied with the results I was getting. Secondly, I resolved that if I only had say 500 messages, classes, or training sessions left in me, I would want to make sure I was in front of the right audience to deliver those messages, classes or training sessions. This was a defining moment in my life because this is when my life as far as ministry is concerned really began to shift and change. Holy Spirit began leading me further away from a traditional church model and I began to focus more on what I was gifted and graced to do that was really producing some results. My response to the question I was asked was the yes Holy Spirit needed in order to move in my life according to the will and intent of the Father. A lot of people are saying yes to God but it is not a specific yes according to the intent of God. Our answers and response to the Father should be conditioned by Holy Spirit. We know not what to pray for as we ought. We can't even say Jesus is Lord without the leadership and guidance of Holy Spirit (1 Corinthians 12:3).

George Washington Carver was a man who believed in prayer and I love to share his story. During a time in his life when George Washington Carver sought a purpose in life, he began to ask God questions about the purpose of the universe and the purpose of man to which God did not give any favorable responses. George Washington Carver became frustrated and sarcastically as if he was mocking God said, "well if You are not going to tell me the answer to those questions then what is the purpose of a peanut?" In response to this question, God spoke to George Washington Carver for days about the peanut. George Washington Carver would combine his lab with his prayer room and Holy Spirit streamed revelation into his heart about the peanut. The rest is history as George Washington Carver went on to discover many different uses for the peanut.

I love sharing this story because it reveals how kingdom communications work. Many times what we are asking, seeking or inquiring is off base with the intent and or will of God and therefore we are not able to satisfy the legal requirements of righteousness or create kingdom life systems that can produce and reproduce kingdom results. We do not know what to pray for as we ought. Therefore all communications with the Home Country must be guided and conditioned by Holy Spirit. The story also serves to reveal a kingdom model. Upon his discovery of something he was appointed to do, George Washington Carver set things in order to accommodate the consistent flow of revelation he had tapped into. And, by means of making a commitment of time, energy and focus, he also set things in order to support what he discovered he was appointed to do. These are all steps we must complete in the process of establishing a kingdom system.

As we conclude this course I pray that you've discovered your peanut and are now asking the right questions and giving the answers that will be the yes Holy Spirit needs in order to move in your life according to the intent and the will of the Father. The next step is to commit something to the decisions you've made. Whatever discoveries you've made pertaining to the will of God for your life that have led you to a place of understanding what you are appointed to do, set those things in order and commit time, energy, focus and any other relevant resources to the fulfillment of those appointed things. Follow the George Washington Carver model and create a kingdom system that reproduces kingdom results. Don't miss the mark and fall short of the glory of God. God will hold each of us accountable for everything He has appointed. Writing and publishing this training course was appointed and therefore a legal requirement that had to be satisfied in order for me to see the kingdom of God manifest in specific areas of my life. As I got closer to completing this project, I began to feel a real push to get this done as Holy Spirit began to reveal all of the opportunities, doors and provision that was tied to this one appointed thing. The kingdom of God is waiting on us to do the things we are appointed to do (1 Peter 3:20). Now is the time to make moves that serve to create a set time that will meet the appointment of God. There is an appointment waiting on you!

ABOUT THE AUTHOR

As a teacher, trainer, mentor and coach, Rodney D. Veney has impacted the lives of many who have positioned themselves to receive from the rich investment of grace in his life. Rodney established the Clarity Training Institute and Leadership Academy in order to serve emerging kingdom leaders throughout the regions in which he is appointed to serve. The Clarity Leadership Academy is an innovative model that utilizes Social Media platforms, webinars, mobile apps and other internet based platforms to serve leaders outside of the local region. Rodney is passionate about serving the intent of God to empower leaders in the discovery and development of their gifts and grace in order to become ultra-productive in the will of God. Rodney brings an Aaron-like #2 grace into the lives of the leaders he serves. He believes the greatest manifestation of his grace shows up as he serves behind the scene of those he is appointed to serve. For more information on the Clarity Leadership Academy, leadership training, mentoring or coaching programs, send an email to wvlegacy@gmail.com. We would love the opportunity to serve you.

Made in the USA
Middletown, DE
22 September 2022